Rivka Léah was born in Eng
graduate in Social Anthropology a.
herbalist. She recently left London to live on the edge of
Dartmoor, South Devon, where she teaches Yoga classes and
runs healing workshops. She is co-founder of the Sacred
Vision foundation for divine consciousness, the purpose of
which is to help men and women gain enlightenment, with
special emphasis on transcending patriarchal programming.

At the age of 27 she met her first spiritual teacher, a
powerful sorceress (and mother), who, despite Rivka's lack
of humility, anger and resistance to a woman sage, still managed to instill right consciousness into her.

Rivka then undertook extensive study and practice of
Yoga both in Britain and the United States, which led her to
her second female teacher, an Avatar (descent of spirit into
form), who travels the world connecting people to their
divine source through the healing power of her voice and
touch.

Rivka is the mother of three small children, a practicing herbalist, teacher, writer, poet and Priestess of the Sacred
Woman's tradition. She is also known by her Indian spiritual
name, Gaitri Devi.

ECSTATICA

Rivka Léah

ECSTATICA

Woman's Realms Of Power

Illustrations by Innocentia Chance

Sacred Vision Press

ISBN 0 9522769 3 3

Typeset By Mike Freeman
Printed and bound in Great Britain by
The Cromwell Press, Melksham, Wilts.

Sacred Vision Press,
P.O.Box 6
Bovey Tracey,
Newton Abbot.
Devon TQ13 9GF.

Acknowledgements.

I would like to acknowledge with gratitude all the people who have helped me to complete this book. Especial thanks to Innocentia and Clem for their heartfelt illustrations and hard work, for the fabulous cover and their unwavering faith in me. Also to Mike Freeman and Bob Mann for their technical support and positive feedback, to Dagny Bouvier-Gordon and Lesley-Ann Crouch and to all my friends who are patiently waiting to read this book, at long last here is Ecstatica.

Ecstatica

You are God's love.
Being present.
Before you start the day.
Meditate to find the answer.
The wisest choices may not always be the easiest
options.
Prayer.
Trust.
Focus.
The choice is yours.
Help me to stop the pain.

<u>INTRODUCTION</u>

Ecstatica is the modern holy woman's handbook. It unlocks the door to the powerful healing force of female ecstasy. Gaining this knowledge is the most urgent task for women today, because it is only ecstatic female energy that will heal the spiritual damage that has been done to the Earth and all her creatures, by the overemphasis of the male principle. This book is a guide to breaking through the fear and negative programming that inhibits our joy. It is a manual for reclaiming our power as women. For restoring the rightful energy that has been stolen from us by the force of consensus against us. The unspoken assumption, enforced with psychic sanction, that we be good girls and do only what is required of us to maintain the status quo - the boring, draining, sleepy, stupid status quo, that leaves some rich and unhappy and others poor and unhappy, and all psychically at war with each other over the slightest thing.

It is a book for women who are too wise and mature to be dictated to by the spoilt and babyish behaviour that characterises and accompanies the world that we are expected to inhabit. It will help you to step out of your unseen mould and to recover your missing filaments, those parts of yourself that you have yielded up, in order to keep the order intact.

This book will take you to the threshold of your own glorious "otherworld". To the place where you can design your own life with unlimited creativity. The rest is then up to you.

Introduction

Through your fear, or your need to be approved of, or your need to be noticed and loved by an unloving world-when it appeared to you to be the only world there was - you have allowed the most crucial parts of yourself, your heart and your feelings, to switch off, to go off drifting in a fog. You have temporarily mislaid your spirit. But it will come back to you. The intentions of this book are to help you to heal yourself, to accelerate your soul's growth, and to re-discover your source and seat of power, your divine inspiration that will lead you onwards on your exciting, ever unfolding path to cosmic bliss.

Ecstatica is a handbook for post-patriarchal consciousness, to stir and inspire us to new ways of being in the world. Ways that are joyful and spiritual and free us from suffering because they do not create debts of negative karma.

It is a practical guide for women to living in love consciousness.

You are encouraged to be brave enough to face your fear and pain, and to look without shunning the truth (which habit builds up lies and illusion, that are ultimately harder to break), at the ways in which we women still continue to support and perpetuate the patriarchal order. Patriarchy still exists, only because we permit it to do so, by means of our suffering and our negativity, which provide fuel for that reality.

We are not using our power constructively. We are squandering and wasting our precious energy, draining ourselves and other women and changing nothing at the core of life. It is no longer acceptable to apportion blame for our misery to others. In order to become free, we must start to take responsibility for our own lives.

Ecstatica

Ecstatica is a feminist sorceror's handbook. It proves that there are other realities to be chosen and lived. Post-patriarchal consciousness is a fact. It is in being right now. Ecstatica is a system of knowledge, a clear ascent to Womanpower, which provides us with the firm conviction and the foundation on which to build the unshakeable faith that is necessary if we are to start to live our lives in unblemished happiness and wholeness. This is the beauty of the project. It is not someone else's system as are most New Age teachings. It is our own system, uncovered and retrieved from the pure memory banks of our own originality.

Patriarchal reality destroys lives and destroys life. We need to learn how to choose for life. With each choice for life and release of suffering, we topple patriarchy a bit more. Each time we do so, we weaken this old order, which unopposedly crumbles because its roots are anyway so decayed.

This is the task of all radical, loving and holy women today. There is no task more urgent, nor more engrossing than the healing and retrieval of our original natures, that have been deeply tarnished and hurt by the cruelty that drives the patriarchal motor. Ecstatica - the feminist bible for the 21st century, is a woman's map to heaven.

THE BOOK OF GAIA

Chapter 1
The Earth is Besieged.

The Earth is the mother of all the people. She nurtures and protects us, as we nestle into her hills and valleys, her crags and crannies. She supports all life. We, the people, are her children, who take her so for granted, this mother of ours. Many of us unthinkingly abuse her and her first line of children, the trees and plants that grow on her surface, as hair grows on our bodies - always more, always regrowth and regeneration - for as long as we live, or as long as she lives?

Is she now dying, this sacred planet of ours? Have we doomed her to the point of inability to heal her damaged body, which is this precious planet? Her body and her spirit are sick as she bows to man's disgraceful and insane exploitation of her. How much can man's mother take? Can she fight back, or is it too late?

We must take care of the Earth's bloodstream which lies clogged with the waste of her human children, the pollution of our thoughts and deeds. Her veins and arteries, the rivers and ley lines, are foul and stinking, dried-up and eroded, dirty and weakened, no longer able to support the life which depends upon them for its survival. Earth's energy is blocked.

People who live in the city forget what it is to live symbiotically with nature, where nature is eradicated to make way for a synthetic life of tower blocks, offices, shops and neighbourhoods that do not have any green space left. What little space there is, is polluted, drained and dirty from overuse and abuse. There are a number of bedraggled plants and animals that live close to humans in a semi-wild state within the city, such as foxes, squirrels and pigeons, scavenging in human debris for their survival. They too are far from their original, wild natures as they attempt to adapt to life in the urban jungle.

Human beings are asleep. Our eyes are simply not open to the awesomeness of the planet we live on, inhabited as it is by myriad species of life besides ourselves. City dwellers are cut off from this knowledge. This is why they cannot relax and release their tension when they get out into the wilderness, and they sit in the safety of their cars at spots of power and healing, or they pollute the fragrant earth with the smell of sickly scents and cigarette smoke.

Country dwellers tend to take it all for granted. So much for granted that they feel it is quite acceptable, no more than a shame perhaps, to knock down and kill a wild creature that has no idea about human roads. Anyone travelling out of the city on roads anywhere within green land cannot fail to notice the sheer amount of strange, wild beings that lie slaughtered by the roadside, guts spilling out onto the road, left for dead without dignity or respect. Each year the number of wild animals,in woodlands and hills, grows smaller and smaller. It is an outrage, which city dwellers are not even aware of, because they have no idea such wild creatures even exist for real, because their only access to them is in the zoo, where animals are preserved for reference, but do not live in their proper environment.

Of course there are occasions when no one can help hitting an unaware bird or animal as it strays into human "territory", but the sheer way in which we drive, in which we plan our travel, takes no account of creatures that have no understanding of human velocity. Our roads are set up to speed and to kill, and no one seems to think that it is a major priority to conserve our wildlife - certainly not as important as getting there on time - so we simply write them down to the casualty statistics that are the result of human importance.

Well, I say it is disgraceful, but we will all suffer, city and country dwellers alike, because our lives are set up and going very fast in the right direction to eradicate most of Earth's mysterious and wonderful wildlife. It is all very well us sitting there watching our televisions, looking at wildlife survival programmes, but on the road outside our doors the nightly massacre goes on.

I hate the way in which animals are pitted against each other by patriarchal society, thus imposing an artificial animosity, causing a split between the species. For instance horses are used by hunts, to run down and chase foxes to the kill, as are the highly prized and beautiful creatures used to aid the matador to look good when he makes his far from dignified and tormented slaughter of the bull in the ring. These innocent beasts - horses - are used to the detriment of their fellow creatures, and against life, as man's accessory, unwitting accomplices in his violence.

Throw down your weapons and pray to Gaia for your protection.

Most of our countryside is polluted. Damaged beyond recognition of its original beauty. The Earth, like woman, was once original, untainted by human exploitation. No words can do justice to the amazing beauty of some parts of the planet. Powerful places, they are just spectacular beyond belief. These places, that inspire us to rapture and awe are really healing sites that need to be protected at all costs. But we do need to avail ourselves of their energy to recharge our own run down batteries.

Eventually, there comes a time in a person's life when they can no longer live within the relentless pressure of the city, if they are to heal themselves to their fullness. It becomes a huge task just to survive in the city, or in depleted countryside. It is necessary to practice lots of yoga and chanting and relaxation just to remain well under such a rigorous breakdown of the immune system as occurs in urban areas. Pollution stems from many sources:- from traffic, from lack of fresh clean air and water, from eating unfresh foods that have travelled long distances and above all from the negative emotional pollution that happens when so many human beings, with so much mental discharge, are crammed into so small a space. The airwaves are jammed. Even meditation cannot truly heal us in such an environment, because there is not really any depth of space and silence to access, and it is necessary to use music or chant to cover this noise up. It becomes hard work just to break even on a healing score.

Ultimately, there is nothing else to do but to leave our cities. To go to these healing grounds, these places of regeneration and power, and even to make our lives there. But even once we have made the break from the cities to the wild places, we will still have to contend with the destructive use to which many of these beautiful sites are assigned.

Firing ranges and military bases dominate England's wilderness - Dartmoor, Salisbury Plain, Lulworth Cove. Our scarce and precious sacred healing grounds have been designated for aggressive use, making them inaccessible, dangerous and noisy. This type of sacrilege could only be committed by governments and nations that have given precedence to war over nature. To 'male' activity based on conquest rather than to 'female' being based on nurture and growth. The Greenham women were amongst those who felt so deeply and justifiably outraged and took their protest to the actual site of desecration, where they remained present and demonstrative throughout. These women were instru ~ntal in creating change, and the power of their belief in th of environmental peace was so great and so corre(can be a lesson for us all in faith and perseverance.

However there are Greenham Common type situations going on all over the world to a greater or lesser extent. Recreational use land, of which there is precious little, has been stolen from the people's use and put to private use for destructive purposes.

One example of this is the use of our most ancient and sacred healing grounds for military activity. This is very karmic. Sacred lands are power spots, special earth energy charged sites that give off a healing force, which is intended to regenerate and re-charge our own energies and to help us to reach a state of inner silence. But when Gaia's gift has been stolen by military powers in the mistaken belief that their needs supercede these healing needs, then we must know we have taken the wrong road. What we have agreed upon, is the setting up of a world based on fear and mistrust, that overshadows the truly protective force that emanates from the sacred grounds.

Those imbued with true faith would know that far greater protection, although less immediately visible, can be invoked by meditation on the Creator's awesome power as it manifests most strongly in these healing sites.

This is why it is not enough any longer for the rest of us to leave protest to the Greenham women. All women must become like Greenham women, in the struggle to take back our Earth and re-designate her as to her primary use - a safe and beautiful home for all her children to share. Then if there is any left over, which there will probably not be, when we have all received our share of necessary food, space and air, then and only then can we let the boys play. Although once they have truly tuned into the beauty of the skylark's song, or the awesome screech of a buzzard soaring over the moors, and the crystal splash of the clear waterfalls, once they have opened their hearts to the pleasures and sweetness of the Earth, they may no longer feel the need to roar their power at the cost of other's oblivion.

We women need to lead the way, by rectifying our everyday choices, even down to the smallest things. Then to be assured that we are not contributing to the warped reversals that are currently considered rational thought in terms of how our Earth is divided up and used. After all if we are not part of the solution, then it follows that we must be a part of the problem. So it is up to us, each and every woman who genuinely requires peace in her lifetime, to ensure that she does not carry out actions that originate in a state of anger. Perhaps those of us who campaign so vigorously for peace should first ensure our own peacefulness.

Lack of awareness is no longer a valid excuse. It is crucial to be brave enough and humble enough, and grateful (to the creativeness that creates all life), for each one of us to dig deep down into our consciousness and to be prepared to examine where we contribute to wrongness - i. e. destruction and suffering. We are always so busy, so stressed, that it is terribly easy to make avoidances, to take short cuts that appear to save time, energy and resources. But if we were to follow through the consequences of our thoughts and actions, we would perhaps see that in the long run we are saving nothing and that we are in effect building up a major problem, by sweeping the mess under the carpet.

The next chapter will consider our environmental attitude and actions, and offer some suggestions of specific ways in which we, as women and consumers, can stop wreaking destruction on ourselves and our environment.

If we do not like soldiers blasting our nature spots to pieces, if we and our children and animals are shocked and disturbed by the scream of low flying jets through our hills and valleys, then we need to be equally sure that we too are not in any way contributing to that thought plane of anger upon which earthly realities are set up. By changing our inner worlds to worlds of peace, each and every one of us, then it will naturally follow that the world will become more peaceful and more holy, as the example of the Greenham women has already shown us.

Chapter 2
Women and The Environment.

Women who do too much

It is time that we saw we are making a massive contribution to the destruction of our own environment by our everyday decisions of what to buy for ourselves and our families. Women are the main purchasers. We are the primary shoppers. We are massive consumers of products and it is therefore critical that we start to give some more thought to what we buy.

For instance almost everything we can buy in most supermarkets contains unecessary ingredients - additives and packaging. We buy tons of things like baked beans, which contain sugar, and almost everything has salt, sugar - in any of its forms - and even vitamins, added. We shouldn't be fooled by the slogans. No artificial additives does not follow that a product is healthy. Most processed foods still require additives that are not good for you. We must start to read ingredient labels and ask - do we really need this? Is it nutrition?

Because we are always so pressured, there is always so much to do with a family, and we tend to take on things we do not have time for, we feel a need to take what we believe are short cuts. As we hurry around trying to perform the Superwomanly task of juggling our work and our home lives, we become great consumers of convenience food products. But what we are actually sacrificing in order to save time, is content. Because the majority of convenience foods are dead foods. They contain no live energy, no vitality. So they do not nourish. All we are doing when we eat such foods is filling up our bodies, but we are not eating anything to rebuild or heal ourselves with. Moreover most convenience foods will actually make us sick, because they are so empty of nutrition that they actually leach vitamins, minerals and fluids from our body in the energy they take to digest.

Only fresh organically grown foods are life-affirming and health creating. No processed or refined foods can possibly do anything but cause us and our families illness. Besides which, the amount of packaging food manufacturers feel they have to use in order for us to buy the product is wasteful. But we should not entirely blame the manufacturers. It is we who are buying the stuff. It is with our "needs" that Lord Sainsbury has become one of the richest men in Britain. We are supporting the manufacturers and the retailers with our demands for consumption. It is something to think about.

This Fragrant Earth

It is important that we women become clear about our responsibility in the future of our environment. We are massive consumers of chemicals and a huge chemical industry has built up around our supposed needs. Our need for cleanliness and hygiene has cause untold damage to the environment in terms of the massive development of suitable toxic substances to rid us of "unfriendly" germs. Bacteria and dirt are considered by us, or so the marketing men tell us, to be the most loathesome things we could ever encounter as we endlessly wage our housewives war on them. We spend masses of money on chemicals and synthetic substances and a whole industry has grown up out of those created needs.

We prop up most of this industry by our need to make invisible those things which we have been taught not to see as nice. Such things as our own bodily scents and exudations - our discharges, our menstrual blood, our sweat, our spots. Our paranoia around these dreaded facets of womanhood causes us to spend vast amounts of money, to pay patriarchal industry to develop and manufacture products that we think will free us and make us sweet. We have really fallen for the anti-woman values that are the basis of the feminine sanitization industries.

The current advertising for tampons, the first time in history that tampons have actually been considered advertisable on television, promotes them as giving a free and easy lifestyle to the wearer. If you use these products, the patriarchal thinking goes, you will hardly notice your periods and more than that you will still be able to be sporty and active. It admonishes young women to cover up their basic bodily functions. Remember these women have not been menstruating very long anyway and the campaigns are targeted at girls who have reached a new phase of womanhood.

We are not saying to them - "hey young women, celebrate your womanhood, enjoy your cycle, let us have a ritual around your first blood." We are not telling them that it's OK to relax and rest when you have your period. That it's a time to dream and let go. We are certainly not opening them to the power and energy that accompanies a woman's period. No indeed! What we are actually saying is, you needn't pay a blind bit of notice to the fact you are menstruating, let Tampax do that for you and you go and play. This is woman-diminishing and encourages them to be ashamed of their secretions, which are seen as a distraction and disturbance to "normal", i.e. period-free life. This is an absolute prescription for disaster to encourage young women to be so cut off from their sacred bodily functions, and is an invitation to later menstrual irregularities, gynaecological troubles, difficulty in birthing matters and inability to be empowered by menopause. Moreover the marketing of such toxic materials as are used to make tampons is not only spiritually wrong for young women, but is downright environmentally irresponsible. Whilst they are promoted as sterile, in order to combat the perceived unhygienicness of periods, tampons do in fact contain magnesium, boron, aluminium, surfactants, acids, alcohols, waxes, amines and hydro-carbons as well as dioxin from the bleaching process. Such a deadly combination of pollutants in one's mouth would be intolerable. Why then do we consider that it is OK to put such deadly substances in our vaginas?

It is a fact that we continue to try to seal up the discharges of our healthy bodies with disgusting chemical messes that poison our land and clog our seas, cause terrible distress and suffering to the animals they are tested on and make us accomplices, albeit unwitting, in the destruction of our own quality of life, and ultimately our planet. We have to see we are being duped and we must start to take over the function of our own menstruation and deny the huge profits to the woman-cleansing industries. Profits that are made out of our bodily functions and our subsequent detachment and alienation from them. Profits that are made for men, at the huge, unredressable cost of wildlife, marine life, laboratory creatures,and women's health. Do we really need this monster built up around our supposed needs? Look at the karma our ignorance and bodily paranoia is creating. Let's wrest our menstruation out of the hands of the scientists and entrepreneurs of the chemical industries.

Worse even than the industry that we have supported around our menstruation, is our massive consumption of perfume. We call it scent and think it is attractive and sexy to mask our natural smell with a highly concentrated synthetic one. We buy it for our loved ones for special occasions and because it is so expensive, the possession of it can even be linked to our status. If it bears a certain designer name it will carry a premium on the price. The rich and famous endorse its use and lend their name to the perfume industry. What possessed Christian Dior to call his perfume **POISON,** was an exquisite twist of irony, because it is. Perfumes poison the environment and us. So much of the air around us is stagnant with the smell of scent. We have all heard of passive smoking, but what about passive perfume poisoning?

One winter a woman wearing a common brand of sweet perfume came to visit us at my house for tea. She sat on a wooden kitchen chair. The following summer you could still smell the perfume. The same thing happened with a car I once bought second-hand. The steering wheel smelt strongly of after-shave. No matter what I did I couldn't get rid of the smell. These scents are very pungent and lingering and yet we are applying them to our bodies every day. Even pure plant essential oils, which do not have a fraction of the potency of synthetically made perfumes, are only advisable to use once a week or so. But we are building up huge deposits of synthetic perfume on our skins which can only cause irritation, abrasion and possibly cancers.

The effect on our health is devastating. Perfume irritates the lungs and causes breathing problems. It weakens the immune system and is particularly dangerous to babies. There is a great emphasis laid on the dangers of smoking to babies and children, but has anyone thought about the dangers of perfume wearing? Yet how many of us wear the stuff habitually, when we go out, in order to attract others or simply boost our own confidence. What is perfume? Isn't it more than just a scent? Women come to depend on it, as they do on make up. But have we really thought about why we feel the need to apply synthetic scent? Isn't the same bodily paranoia that pervades the menstruation industry at its root? We must stop buying into such a useless and dangerous industry. It is purely a vanity industry, and does nothing to further the good of anyone concerned save the manufacturers. The profits are beyond imagination. There is a spylike secrecy that goes on at the design stage, where perfumes are dreamed up for us. A terrible egoistic fuss is made about the creation and blending of perfumes.

The clean Earth has the most fragrant scent about her. The grass, the fields, the forests, the glades possess exquisite perfumes that we can deeply inhale into our lungs, evoking emotions, memories, and bringing deep healing. There is nothing so toxic as air thick with the synthetic sickliness of perfume wearing women and men. As they pass you their forced scent lingers in the whole environment, completely masking nature's scent. This is even worse when you have climbed up to a natural beauty spot to breathe in its fresh fragrance, and your lungs are really open. But it invariably occurs.

Natural perfumes from flower blossoms, of hay and horses, in fact any pleasant natural scent can invoke all sorts of responses in the emotions and brainwaves. This is the science that aromatherapy is based on. I am sure that this was the original idea behind the creation of perfume, to enhance rather than to mask nature. However, it has become perverted. Pure plant essential oils however, not only contain gorgeous and varied scents, but they also possess wide ranging health benefits. Even more than this, essential oils harmonise and rebalance emotional states. Perhaps because they are so beneficial, women are resistant to changing to their use. Because the vanity aspect is almost minimal with essential oils. Vanity is shallow, and self-serving whereas natural scent is of a healing nature. Two "pretty" scents, not the same thing! Nevertheless one can make fantastic perfumes by blending essential oils. It is fun to experiment and create your own - and above all, it does no-one, especially children, who can benefit from plant essential fragrance oils, any harm.

Massage is just one of the ways of applying essential oils (diluted with a base oil, because they are strong), but there are many and varied uses of essential oils, one of the least medical being as perfume. Neroli and Rose are amongst the most expensive of these, because they are harder to produce, yet they cost a fraction of the price of synthetic perfumes, and are used in the most expensive of the latter to scent. So perfume wearing is just one of those unthought about habits that no longer makes sense for the 21st century, since it adds to the pollution and there is a viable, and in my opinion, infinitely preferable alternative. It's not a question of having to live with your natural smell even. Essential oils have been created by nature for our pleasure and health.

As with all man-made, woman-targeted bathroom necessities, the 21st century message must become heard. Have fun, make your own, save on toxic pollution and don't make those around you sicker. The question is, have we women yet grown to the level of self-confidence and strength where we can accept this as the only intelligent possibility?

Chapter 3
Women and Food.

I have to move to this area of life now in relation to our adverse effect on our environment, because apart from our relationships to men, none is perhaps more disturbed than our relationship to food. · There is no doubt that we have perverted one of life's most important necessities, but also one of life's great pleasures, into a sinful activity.

We eat to live firstly. Anorexic and Bulimic women play on this aspect when they unconsciously threaten others with their self-destructive relationship to food. It is the only power they can gain access to in their current life state. True power of woman has been repressed, this is manifestation of patriarchal power. It is holding power-over, manipulating, threatening, the only power that emotionally beaten women can find. It is a self-pitying, cry for help. I am unloved and therefore I am worthless. I am set into a pattern where I cannot allow myself to be nourished, because I am not good enough. There is deep anger involved. But food is also enjoyable, it can be a rapturous experience to eat wonderful food, and this is the second way women with eating disorders punish, this time themselves, in their denial of the pleasures of eating. By punishing ourselves with our food relationship, we are playing into patriarchal definitions of us as restrained and safe women, because we are cutting off our wildness, and stunting our creativity, as we are stunting our appetites.

In a sense, eating disorders among women are not confined merely to those of us with named perverted appetites. They are the ones who use food, the eating or non-eating of it, as a life and death matter. But many of the rest of us are hung up around the second aspect of food - the enjoyment aspect. How many of us are free enough to display a lusty appetite - with pleasure and with no sense of guilt?

Because the sad fact is we have allowed ourselves to turn food into an enemy. It is obvious that this is the case, because we think that food is going to hurt us. We eat with anger, and we eat out of anger. We also eat out of unfulfilled need. We eat to punish ourselves or to comfort ourselves. If we do eat with pleasure, we will probably punish ourselves for it afterwards.

Dieting is the most common form of punishment - although periods of disciplined eating can be good for your health and self-esteem, and there is nothing wrong with trying to lose some weight if it would make you feel fitter. On the other hand, the massive obsession with dieting and the industry that has grown up around yet more of our created needs is out of all proportion. Moreover it has most certainly encouraged us to name food as the enemy.

Food is not the enemy. Food is an innocent substance that we grow and produce and that willingly supplies us with its energy and nourishment. The warped perspective, whereby we look at food in terms of how fat it is going to make us is ridiculous. Drinking coloured milk shakes instead of eating meals in an effort to get thin means that we have become totally fooled as to the nature of food. The enemy is our own lack of awareness of what, why and how we eat. What is truly at fault are our choices about what we eat, because they do not stem from natural unconditioned hunger responses, but from masses of layers of mental and bodily conditioning around food. Food has ceased to become fun. Even if we are not eating directly poisonous food, which mostly we are, even if we eat good food with anger, guilt or fear, it will become as poison in our system, as it mixes with our harmful thoughts and negative emotions and churns in our guts.

It is this aspect of eating that makes us fat. Not the food. Even dieting means eating with such obsession that we are unlikely to cure the root cause of our problem, which depends upon us re-educating ourselves to eat with awareness and happiness, and to monitor the effects of the food we eat, on our digestions.

We need to ask more questions, like; does a food make us feel well or ill? If so why? Is it the food itself or our attitude towards it? Is there truly pleasure in eating those things that make us feel physically or emotionally bad? Can we really enjoy eating things that have such a complex of thought and emotion accompanying them? I don't think so. Having a secretive, private relationship with food is such an easy form of abuse in a society that sanctions female slimness as beauty.

The thing to do is to start to enjoy eating again and only to eat when you are ready to enjoy yourself. Then to eat with awareness and attention on the food, savouring it, chewing it properly and to stop feeling that it is not your right to enjoy food. Become happy with your body, by being happy in your body. Surface sexuality is about how slim you feel, but it may not be your nature to be thin. In Hawaii and the South Seas big fat Mommas are considered beautiful. But we are living in a society where beauty is only required from the outside, leaving most of us feeling shitty and worthless inside ourselves. But what is the point of trying to look like a saint when you feel like a sinner? The hopeless, destructive lives of many models and starlets show the truth of the sadness of such emptiness.

We are a society of hungry women. We are stuffing ourselves with every filler to heal our emptiness. But our emptiness comes from our own inner torture, our self and other judgements, from our lack of self-esteem and our choices to be victims and to suffer in life, whilst not allowing ourselves to correctly define and experience satisfaction. Our relationships to food simply reflect our inner hunger, as we look to fill up our unhappy lives, substituting food for the love we don't believe we deserve. We are a world of women looking for someone and something external to satisfy us - but we will never, ever, become whole this way. Wholeness can only come from changing our attitudes - to ourselves, to others and to our environment. We have to start taking responsibility for our own pain. We may not have consciously caused it, but we can consciously change it, and that is the important point.

We can start by changing our diets. By learning how to eat foods that make us feel good. Many of us are so divorced from food as a natural product that we could not eat whole foods and enjoy them, because our appetites crave tastes adulterated with salt, sugar or fats. We can learn how to nourish ourselves and the difference between this and eating to starve ourselves which is what eating the wrong foods, in anger, is all about.

Of course the first thing to do is to accept that we do want to nourish ourselves, because if we don't value ourselves, then no amount of dieting will make us feel any better, except on the surface. I accept that losing weight for some women may be a trigger to a self-esteem spiral. But we have to see that for the majority of us, food is a means to fill up our intense longing and yearning for love and fulfilment.

This hunger for fulfilment is actually not true hunger at all. What it is is greed, because it is taking in substances above and beyond the needs of nutrition. Funnily enough it is this type of greed that bears great relation to why a third of the world's population is dying from starvation. Because of our choices, people in Africa do not have enough to eat. We eat foods that we do not need and do not enjoy, yet continue to demand massive production around these non- needs that we still desire so much.

Look for example at female desire for chocolate. We eat so much cocoa and sugar that our industrialists went to the growing countries to get the raw materials, bought up or stole all the land, which might otherwise have been used for subsistence, exploited the natives as workers (or stole their labour as slaves), and made them so desperate to fear their survival that they had to compete with each other for resources thus creating wars and killing.

Meanwhile we continue to buy and stuff the substance with a guilt and secretiveness that makes us ill. The innocent little chocolate bar that we do not really need and yet still desire, rests upon lives and lives of suffering. Please understand, I am not talking about enjoying a little of a pleasurable substance with awareness. I am referring to a vicious circle of eating and despising - which is eating from a state of anger, and is an avoidance act that calls us to look at our true life states and face the pain that makes us behave so destructively.

So too look at our cravings for burgers. It seems as if there is an an ever increasing campaign to wipe out the cultural eating habits of nations as one after the next capital city look to MacDonalds as a model of modernity. Such eating homogeneity bears terrible cost. Not just to the poor, unfortunate beasts that end up minced into pieces, stuffed virtually untasted into most of the world's mouths. There is always such a low switched-off feeling in these plastic, feeding factories. But there is another side to the karma of hamburger eating that is less obvious to the junk food cravers that seek to stuff the pain of their unhappy lives. It takes an acre of grass land to fatten a beef animal. On the same amount of land enough grains can be grown to feed many more people. The animal alone will consume massive quantities of grain to become fat enough to be slaughtered. In a world of scarce resources it makes no economic sense whatever to produce so much beef, when one can grow grains, which are the necessary basic nourishment of humanity, on less land, for less cost and with higher yields. Also, in countries where grass-lands are sparse, local people are being encouraged to pro-duce beef and hence chop down trees and rainforest to do so, with devastating environmental consequences for all of us.

Should we eat meat?

This is one of the big dilemmas of this decade. Many years ago, when food was more locally and simply produced, most people didn't really question what they were putting into their mouths. Now with increased environmental con-cern and the expanding effect of "New Age" consciousness, there is a changed attitude towards vegetarianism. It is gen-erally accepted that to be spiritual you have to give up meat.

I do think it is true that animals suffer when they are slaughtered, even if they are reared compassionately. The most compassionate thing to do is to refrain from eating ani-mal foods, i.e. those that involve deliberately taking the ani-mal's life. However, if we try to overcome or deny our own desires, to the point of becoming unhappy or angry, then we too are in suffering, and neither is this "spiritual" behaviour. If meat is one of those "foods" that heals our damaged emo-tional or physical bodies, perhaps because we have been brought up on it, and we have desire for it, then it is not nec-essarily helpful to stop eating it entirely and suddenly. The correct thing to do is to weigh up the suffering involved and to free your spirit. An unhappy vegetarian is not necessarily helping her spiritual growth. As long as there is desire, then it is important to acknowledge and feed that desire, because that is where one's true freedom and happiness lies. As we connect more deeply and permanently with divine con-sciousness, so we fall more in love with life, and our food cravings and attachments will naturally lessen.

Meanwhile we should eat the food we desire, but with awareness, pleasure and only as much as we need. This acknowledgement, as opposed to deprivation, is the only way to become unhooked from our attachment.

There is no doubt that meat is like a drug in the sense that people can become very compulsive and dependent upon it, taking more than they really need or want, and eating crappily produced and low vitality meat. Many of us who know this, placate ourselves by refusing to eat such wretched animals as end up in a Big Mac and will only eat organic free range beasts. But it is important not to fool ourselves that because it is organic and free range that it doesn't hurt, because there is no such thing as cruelty-free meat - unless of course it died in your path, through no cause of your own. It doesn't seem correct or necessary to take the lives of baby animals or animals still in their prime. If we needed to eat them to survive it would be quite different. But no-one can honestly tell me they needed veal?

Because we are a grassland growing country, certain arguments arise in my mind. If we left the land to grow, we would have masses of naturally growing grasses. Humans cannot eat or digest grass, but grazing beasts like cows and sheep can. In a sense when we eat these animals we get the grass through them. Also animals naturally eat other animals. There is a food chain. I cannot emphatically say that we are not supposed to eat meat. I do not know the answer, if there is one. I think it depends upon how much we need and want to eat it. No one can really say what is right for someone else. The decisions must come from your heart and clear insight. It is probably better not to kill to eat. But only if you are happy with this decision can it be said to be correct. Obviously it is necessary to become aware about what you are shoving in your mouth and where it came from. If you could happily go outside and kill a creature then you have every right to eat it. But if you depend upon your meat

being secretly slaughtered for you in some back-street abba-
toir, cut into nice pieces and presented so that it doesn't look
like an animal, then you are not being entirely honest and
you need to keep the facts in mind when you consume your
emotional drug. Most importantly take no more than you
need.

The karma of food goes on and on. The politics of starvation have the root of greed. Some have not enough
because others have taken far more than they need. To a
large extent, in our daily lives, we women fall into the latter
category. We support and encourage patriarchal industry to
take resources we do not really need. We consume these
resources like hungry animals in the hope that they will
make us feel good, look good or smell good, when deep
down inside ourselves we know that we need none of these
things. Simplicity is the key to our happiness. By learning to
consume only as much as we need for our nourishment and
our pleasure, we will fall back into balance. Then too will
those who do not ever have enough also find balance and
there will still be more than enough for all.

Of course that day is a long way ahead, but we can start
by letting go a little of those attachments that cause us more
pain than pleasure, and by knowing that we are starting to
build true satisfaction in our lives, as we learn to like ourselves more, based on our acts of wisdom and compassion.

What should we eat? So many diets abound in the
health literature of the West, that it can become very confusing indeed to know what to eat and what not to eat in order
to become healthy.

Because everybody is different, one simply must take
into account such factors as constitution and genetic heritage,
when planning one's nutrition. Climate is also incredibly
important, because the heat or coldness of the atmosphere
affects the digestion and transformation of food into energy

in the body. This is why Californians who come over here raving about the benefits of raw food diets, may be advising us unwisely when one takes into account the coldness and dampness of our weather for much of the year. Raw food is cold and wet. It taxes the spleen to digest it. Therefore it is only really suitable in the summer. Eating a raw food diet in the winter in Britain and other cold, damp climates, especially if there is a propensity to dampness in the system, is going to create much weakness and cold in the body. On the other hand,too much heating food may be inappropriate. If there is a person with too much heat in their bodies, who is advised for their health to take garlic and other pungent spices, the excess heat will eventually start to dry up all the bodily fluids and the blood, causing constipation, wrinkled skin and other signs of dehydration.

This is why any diet, to be correct, must take into account the energetic balance and constitution of the person and their external environment. However, there are some basic conditions that apply to the nutrition of human beings no matter where on the globe they may be situated.

Firstly we need to become aware that to be healthy and happy we ought to take the majority of our nutrition from the categories of whole grains, nuts, seeds, fruit and land and sea vegetables. This is a vegan diet which is sensibly balanced and creatively designed to provide most of our health building nutrition. As you get into a diet like this the possibilities just go on and on unfolding. There is no end to the delicious foods that you can create around these staple ingredients. If you feel that this is a very limited selection of foods, I advise you to fast for a day or two and then think again, because you will realise that there are a vast amount of foods to choose from. We are very lucky these days in that there is a growing availability of pre-prepared vegan foods available to buy, which makes it easier to have enough to eat. There are now alternatives to all the animal foods; vegan sausages, burgers, rashers, poultry substitutes, milks, cream, eggs - all of them can be substituted by plant based proteins, which do not build up cholesterol deposits and do not build up karma. There is no need to be a gravelly voiced vegetarian, whose consumption of dairy products threatens to spill up out of their lungs, blocking their noses and throats. We don't need meat for our health either. In fact meat is a decaying,putrefying substance that rots in our digestive system. Eating dead animals in any amount is to deaden, poison and putrefy our bodies for the next 72 hours. It is also totally unecessary to resort to killing for our food in the way that we still do. It is simply unacceptable. It is one thing to hunt for a bit of game or meat, but to consume it in factory produced form, to the massive extent we do is insane for a society that claims to be civilised.

It is not either a question of a moral judgement from God for our sins, when we look at the outcome of all this unbalanced eating. Simply people will become very ill due to the way in which animal products are produced.

Animals reared for food are kept in unhealthy ways. Pig and poultry production particularly is going to create sickness among the animals and those who depend upon them for their food. Where there is suffering, there is always disease. This is indisputable natural law. Happy animals, like happy people, are likely to be sickness free. But animals kept in degradation and fear cannot maintain their immunity. We are going to witness greater and greater breakdowns of health in those humans who consume these products. It goes beyond even the unhealthiness of consuming the animal substance itself, to the fact of consuming such large amounts of toxic energy as is contained within the bodies of such wretched deprived creatures. The practices that go on in food farming in order to produce high yields are many of them polluting and illness creating.

It is one thing to live without meat. More and more

41

people are eating less meat, giving up eating it, or even turning vegetarian. However one of the most important substances in our lives that we need to learn to live without is milk. But the dairy industry is so rooted, and the goodness of milk, its protein and calcium content, so highly marketed and believed in, that this is going to be a goal for the long distant future.

But there will inevitably be illness among dairy consumers. There is already the obvious and simple evidence of the massive mucous and phlegm forming properties of dairy produce. Even drinking a little milk will produce a glob of phlegm in the throat and cause thickening of mucous membranes, blocking up the pipes of the body. Milk contains protein that is very difficult to digest for humans and sometimes the body reacts to this "foreign" protein, by producing antibodies (allergies). But that is again just the unhealthiness of the substance itself, and is as nothing compared to the spiritual aspects of milk consumption, which we cannot allow ourselves to remain switched-off from and unaware of any longer. This is especially relevant to women, because we too are milk producers for our own young, and it is time we started to extend our compassion to other female creatures and to realise that the brutality they endure under patriarchy is only relative to, but no different from our own.

Lactation is a female prerogative and a female concern. We produce milk to feed our young. When we are pregnant our hormones develop, so that we, and we alone, become capable of nurturing and nourishing our babies for the first few months. It is exactly the same with cows. They can only produce milk because they have given birth. But when you see a field of cows with full udders, do you ask where are their babies? Where are the calves of the dairy cows who come trudging home to be milked, hardly able to walk because of the distension of their breasts? Is it a natural thing for a female whose baby is no longer with her to be kept in artificial milk production, stimulated by milking machines to produce milk for twice daily milking?

Anyone who has breast-fed a baby, or been around a mother who has, may know what it is like to be engorged, or to have mastitis. The natural way of healing such painful conditions is for the baby, who feeds little and often, to relieve the distention. But cows are divorced from their natural state. There are no calves to suckle and yet they are still producing milk. This is a recipe for disaster to those who steal and consume milk that is not intended for them. They are taking babies' food that they do not need. They are drinking wrongness and that wrongness is in the forced production of the substance. We are all doing it, all over the world. We are causing distress and unhappiness to mother cows, which we neither need to do, and certainly as the evidence to our health shows, must not continue to do. I beseech all women, all over the planet, to become aware of the risks to health of dairy consumption and to protect lactating creatures by linking and identifying with them as mothers. We need to stop buying into and depending upon the dairy industry men to nurture our children. There are healthier and uncruel alternatives to the countless yoghurts we stuff our children with. Their constantly runny noses should be enough incentive to wean us off cows' milk consumption. Anyone who still needs more reason to learn to live without milk should take themselves off down to the country for the day and look at some dairy cows coming in to be milked and tell me that they feel this is the right and happy way for animals to live. It is quite a different matter to take a little of an animal's milk, while leaving her enough to feed her babies. But the babies need to be the priority, not us.

Many people feel that they need some other form of protein than a vegan based diet can provide from time to time. It may be that occasional fish or even meat is needed, especially during periods of stress to the body or increased energy needs like in pregnancy. In this case one should not feel it is wrong to take from the animal, in the right spirit of gratitude. But it is a question of only taking from animals the amount one needs. This is different from taking for greed, which is what life in the West is based upon, with no gratitude or respect for the life of the animal. This kind of mindless killing and pillaging is not something that will be able to go on and on ad infinitum. It is just too ignorant and too sick-making. As more and more people become polluted-out with meat and animal products, we can expect to see changes. But there is no doubt that whole nations are deeply addicted to meat and are only able to see a substitute in cheese and eggs.

It is therefore better to eat fish, should one feel the need to take in a denser form of protein. I am not saying that there is no suffering in the kingdom of the seas. It is not a question of consuming masses of tinned tuna, or farmed salmon or boiling live lobsters or eating fish fingers made from mixed minced fishes hauled from over fished waters. But a little local, simple fish can provide the Yang energy we need to feel complete. I do not know if fish feel the same pain and terror that mammals feel when their lives are sacrificed for human food. But it may anyway be quite wrong to eat animals bigger than ourselves. Most seas are now dirty and polluted from human waste and chemicals. Eating organic fish from clean waters is something we may not be able to do for ever as the seas become more polluted and lifeless. But eating scallops, oysters and other shellfish probably engenders a lot less suffering than cheese, milk and egg production. If one is not ready or happy to become completely vegan, fish-eating in small quantities is still healing to the body. Fish however tends not to be an emotional body food, which is why people are somewhat less greedy and addictive about it, which has to be a better thing.

The basic staple food of the human diet however must be composed of whole grains. We in the West have become totally removed from the basis of the natural human diet, which is cereal in nature.

A very small proportion of people eat grains in the way that the body requires for its fuel and well-being. Most of our carbohydrate needs, in this country at least, are provided by potatoes, because they are cheap and easy to produce and fill us up. But whilst the occasional potato can be a nourishing and pleasant food, potatoes in quantity are actually quite poisonous to the system and extremely constipating. They come from the Nightshade family of plants and cause terrible bloating as they absorb our bodily fluids in their digestion. Occasionally British people will cook a whole grain, usually a pan of brown rice, but the majority of the nation know nothing about the use of other grains, or how to cook and eat them. Apart from rice, which needs to be very well cooked in plenty of water until it is soft enough to be digested properly, there is also millet, which is good for those with a weak digestion as it helps the spleen. It is a yellow grain that re-balances the earth element, which is often so disturbed in women. Nurturing is an aspect of the earth element, which rules the spleen, and which controls menstruation and affects lactation. Yellow foods, like corn, another cereal, (also pumpkins, bananas, carrots, sweet potatoes and yams etc), contain Vitamin A and are very nourishing for women and children.

Buckwheat is a tonic grain to strengthen the kidneys with a distinct taste. It can be roasted or baked with vegetables. Barley is a demulcent - it provides fluids - which is strengthening and laxative. It counteracts poisons in the body.

Wheat is the least digestible of grains, yet the most widely available. The majority of breakfast cereals are wheat based and cause irritation and bloat to the stomach. If we were to try to live without bread most of us would probably die from starvation, so great is our dependency upon this form of wheat consumption. Nevertheless this is what more and more people are having to do, so sick are they becoming from the intake of wheat products. Because of the phlegm wheat eating creates, many are sick with candida (a yeast overgrowth in the gut), and can no longer tolerate yeast or wheat products. They, and we all, need to look to other grains for our survival.

The Scottish have always known about the strengthening and warming content of oats, because they grew and consumed oats in large quantities. But it is also a fact that oats relax and soothe the nervous system, and contain calcium and protein. They can be eaten without milk and instead of wheat flours. Oat flakes make a good binding for puddings and children generally love them.

So with grains as our staple, by combining them with seeds or pulses, we make a plant protein that is far healthier, more digestible but as nutritious as animal protein sources.

Pulses include lentils, and legumes, such as peas and beans, especially mung beans, aduki, black eyed, soya, haricot, turtle, butter, kidney, flageolet and so on as well as chick peas and green beans, like french, runner and broad, to name just a few of the wide variety available to us today. There are also the soya based proteins like Tofu, Tempe and Miso that fall into this category.

Seeds include sesame, sunflower and pumpkin, either roasted or pureed and made into a spread. Or seeds of any variety can be sprouted and eaten, whereby the starch turns into natural sugar and the vitality and energy of eating living food is contributory to health and well-being. It is also fun to grow one's own food, and seed sprouting makes the ideal green fingered exercise for city, gardenless flat dwellers as well as increasing their health under such adverse circumstances.

There is also the world of nuts to look to. Almonds particularly contain abundant calcium and can be made into a delicious milk substitute. Nuts contain protein and fat. People tend to see nuts as fattening, but that is when they are treated as a between meat-meals snack. Too much fat and protein in that type of diet leads to putrefaction in the gut, overweight and constipation. People who eat meat certainly should not take nuts as well.

On the other hand, nuts are an essential and delicious form of sustenance to a plant eating person. There is nothing like a home made nut roast to rival the Sunday joint. On the other hand the microwaved frozen specimens that many pubs serve up to appease the vegetarian guests are very off-putting indeed, even to vegetarians. But then many pub landlords when asked "what's the nut roast like"? will turn up their noses and say, "I hate the stuff". This is just one of those types of thinking one encounters as a vegan trying to be "normal".

Indeed amongst the problems of adhering to a vegan diet in a predominantly meat-eating culture, the issue of being able to go out and enjoy a social life figures strongly. It can be very hard to have a sociable life, when enjoyment appears to centre exclusively around imbibing animal prod-ucts - Cappucinos, Steak Bars, even vegetarian restaurants that simply substitute cheese and eggs for meat. No one wants to have to stay in all the time, or to have to take their own foods everywhere, or to be a problem guest to friends.

This is why people join the Vegan Society and quite rightly too, because these brave pioneers need support, knowledge and inspiration. Vegans, who have learnt how to cook well, need to open cafes and restaurants where hedo-nism is still a priority. Too many vegetarian restaurants still provide cramped, rushed conditions where it is impossible to sit and enjoy a leisurely meal or snack. Most vegetarian restaurants, because they can resort to cheese and eggs for protein, do so and their cooks use little creativity to cater for vegans. Therefore whilst they avoid the karma of killing ani-mals, they do not withdraw themselves from the world of cruelty farming. Moreover they are not even putting their energies into the health aspects of vegetarian diet.

Indeed it is a sad fact that there are many vegetarians who are amongst the most unhealthy people. Vegans, on the other hand, or those who eat fish rather than dairy foods, tend to be very healthy. Although there are those that do not take the trouble to eat properly balanced diets, many vegans are amongst the wisest and most creative eaters on the planet today.

It would be wonderful if every town supported a vegan restaurant, where one could not only go to eat socially, but also to get inspiration and encouragement for continuing to live in the spiritual way that is so obviously liberating. Having been a meat-eater and animal dependent consumer can be hard to let go of. However there can be nothing to parallel the energy that one gains from the release of one's karmic ways, and the freedom of spirit that ensues, once one has made the decision to live in accord with natural law, as it manifests in the pull of our consciences and shows us the right way ahead.

It is an urgent mission to start freeing ourselves from our dependencies, because it is these needs that cause imbalance in our bodies and in the production and distribution of natural resources. It is the over-consumption of nature, without thinking of replacement in the future, and the refinement of natural things into products, that has already brought many of the creatures and plants of the earth to the brink of extinction.

How much more destruction are we prepared to take responsibility for? Because make no mistake, it is our material dependencies that are turning our glorious earth from a paradise into a wasteland. Ranging from our intake of excessive animal products through to the over-manufacture of chemicals for our hygiene and cleanliness, all of these things are unecessary to our health and well-being. In fact our material dependencies are positively destructive to our health, they cause disease. Our happiness must come from within our own depths to be true.

We must realise that in feeding these external needs, most which have been created by patriarchal minds, either directly, or by inventing the psychological pressures upon us in order to sell the product, we are feeding the patriarchy in its greedy hell-bent quest to wipe us out by destroying the fragile planet we walk on. But we must take responsibility, because it will be the ignorants' loss as well as ours. Whether they thank us or not in the end is unimportant. What matters is that we begin by facing up to our painful attachments and desires, and simplify our lives. It is only in this way that we can free ourselves from the patriarchal stranglehold over our lives, as we bring back new life to our lovely mother Earth.

Raspberry Leaf

Motherwort

Birthroot

Squaw Vine

THE BOOK OF MARY

Mary was the mother of God's child, Jesus. Popular myth (the Bible) has decreed her to be a virgin mother, that is one who has become pregnant without having had sexual intercourse with the baby's father. Thus the God of the Bible has used Mary to incubate and birth "his" child,like some kind of surrogate mother, who is only too willing to bear the fruits of patriarchy's continuance. As a woman and a mother, I find the idea of virgin birth very offensive, because it takes reproductive control out of the hands of women and suggests that they might be no more than vehicles for the production and creation of children. Her will is not directly involved. This Mary is a very un-powerful role model for women. Gabriel comes to her and asks her to bear God's son - she willingly complies. Why? Is it because it is such an honour to bear God's son that she renounces her own womanly needs and biological functions?

Christianity has sinned against women, by denying Mary the earthy and pleasurable activity of lovemaking as a necessary pre-requisite to becoming pregnant. Mary may

51

have been pure, but she cannot have been a literal virgin, and a mother.

Revisioning Mary means seeing her as an independent woman, the mother of a divine child, creatress and first sacred teacher of that infant, but not merely a channel, an empty vessel for his incarnation. As a loving mother and a compassionate saint, it is as much Mary's energy and attributes that go into the creation of that child, equally of course with the biological father. The true Madonna is the ecstatic mother, the one who is deep in the bliss of love for her child and her lover/partner, in the full knowledge and acceptance that they have, with God's will, created a child.

Chapter 1
Healing the Unborn.

MOTHER -'A female or thing that creates, nurtures, or protects something... a female who has given birth to off-spring.' (*Collins New English Dictionary*).

What is motherhood? The general consensus is to view it as a social role and a biological function which occurs once a female procreates.

I seek to offer a broader definition of motherhood which stems from the spiritual aspect of being in relationship to creation. Motherhood is a state that awakens women to their healing potential. It is a very sacred state. When we give birth to offspring - the physical and physiological factor - we also give rise to a new emotional level of being, a state of higher awareness triggered by our entrance into a new mode of life. As that infant leaves its mother's body, be it easily or with great resistance and difficulty, so she is suddenly opened to the flow of raw emotion that accompanies that separation, be it joyous or painful, or as it is in many cases, a mixture of both. To become a mother is to become tender and vulnerable, as it is to become inspired and infused with the joy of the life force. But to be a mother is also a restructuring of relationships. Not only between those closest to her, but to all those around her, and to the Earth itself. Because to become a mother is to be in relationship to our planet either as healer or destroyer, as every choice we make for our children is a choice not only for their future, but for the future of the Earth. It is that cut and dried, whether or not we choose to become aware of it, and there are no half measures. Whilst the ship is definitely sinking, there is hope in the fact that it has not yet gone down.

This book is for mothers everywhere. For all those females of every species, who are engaged in the creation and protection of life. From the greatest of all, Mother Earth nurturing her Earthlings, down to the tiniest mother duck devotedly protecting her ducklings, we are all engaged in the same life task, that of birthing, rearing and protecting our young. The Earth cannot read this book, but she can feel our thoughts and suffer the results of our actions. Neither can the mother duck read, but her babies can thrive due to the care and compassion of her human sisters, in educating their children to become ecologically aware human beings. A human mother can relate to a mother of any species, once she realises that under patriarchal values, all mothers are under threat of diminishment and that the protection of one's young, is for any species a very challenging task.

There are some species who have no choice in the matter. They are simply not allowed to rear their young. These are the species who have been assigned for man's use . Required to breed and surrender her young, the dairy cow is bred from every year in order to ensure constant lactation, and profit for her owner. As I said, when talking about our nourishment in the previous chapter, as long as human desire for animal milk is so high, there is little hope that the baby calf will be permitted to spend its infancy rightfully at its mother's udder. The passion of a mother cow licking her young calf is a sight to behold, yet it is scarcely seen. The peaceful image of contented English cows grazing away a summer afternoon is a myth. Cows are in fact under the eternal bondage of twice daily machine milking. Year after year they are forced to surrender their newborn calves, who are dragged away crying mournfully. If they are males they may be destined for veal. If they are females they will be artificially reared on, ironically, powdered formula cows' milk, fed from a bucket or a rubber teat, until they too are old enough to start the cycle of breeding themselves. I know this because

I have worked in livestock farming. I have milked cows and reared their calves, and I know what goes on.

Some unfortunate babies are prized for their warmth and cuddliness. This is why they are made into coats. Human mothers should be able to relate to the sad eyed mother seal, whose pups are dragged brutally from her side. Because as a mother who is unable to protect her young any longer she is a mother de-powered. This is happening everywhere on our planet. Mothers of every species are being used to reproduce and surrender their young, not just for man's need, but for humankind's greed. Millions of mother creatures see their young die every day, not only for human food, but for human pharmaceutical experimentation, expensive accessories - particularly female targeted ones - and just for what some humans misguidedly term pleasure - cubhunting.

All of us who have experienced giving birth, or who can empathise with those who have, know the vulnerability and tenderness that accompanies that state. Close to the source of creation, mothers are in a special state of power. Bestowed with the ability to love unconditionally, new mothers enter a state of grace, an ecstatic connection to the source of all existence.

But motherhood is a double edged sword. It also opens us up to all the suffering and sadness of our fellow/sister/daughter creatures. Motherhood gives us the power to feel our feelings with greater intensity. (The tendency to dull this heightened sensitivity with alcohol and drugs, or to pollute it with negativity, stress, guilt and depression, represents a major draining of the force of new motherhood. It is an almost impossible feat for a new mother to enjoy her postnatal bliss, without being "brought back down to earth" by someone, if not herself. There is more about this later). This is why we must demand our right to the experience of our rightful bliss. It is the force we can enjoy that serves to balance out the pain and suffering of our fellow creatures, that we are forced to witness. It is one of the most powerful healing forces on this Earth. This energy bestowed upon us with the release of our baby into the world - literally, deliverance accompanies delivery - is a mystical and sacred power. Hindus call it Anant Vayu, the energy that flows through the mother after conception until birth. It is the source of the elation that enables pregnant and birthing women to feel such profound happiness and peace. It is the source of our inspiration, our raw material and it is ours to experience and immerse ourselves in, whilst it lasts. None should try to usurp it, and everyone coming within its orbit should respect it because at this time the mother is closely connected to the source of creation and has the unconditional lovingness of a saint.

I have been in this ecstatic state three times, with the birth of my three children, and I have come to understand how, under the system in which we live, we squander and surrender it. This is because we do not understand it, in the first place, but also because our training and conditioning leaves us so unprepared for the rapturousness of birth which we are led to believe is a fearful and traumatic event. I'm not saying it isn't painful, it can be and often is, but the dreadful fear we have of pain, albeit not a pathological pain, allows us to sell ourselves so short, that we would trade our most passionate moments for some pain relief. Our hatred of pain, even in childbirth, would allow us to dull our most exquisite sensibilities, and of course we are aided in this by the medical profession who control the notion of childbirth as a medical, and therefore an unpleasant and certainly **NOT** a blissful experience.

The elemental force and power of childbirth is truly woman's ally. She can ride the waves of this force with balance and rhythm and emerge at the other end of the process whole, joyous, invigorated. Or, under another scenario, she can resist the waves, allow them to batter and exhaust her body, become swamped with doubt and fear about her own strength and confidence, with the result that she finally crashes, panics and cries out for helpers to come into her most intimate moment, her most private space and bail her out. She has thus squandered her moment of power and allowed her precious connection with herself to be brutally prised apart , as likely as not, by those who have no thought for her emotional satisfaction with herself.

Because it was she who did this - and ultimately no-one else, the power is there for the taking - she probably hates herself. She may psychologically beat herself up about it. Maybe she also beats up other women about it too! Especially those who she thinks have done better than her. Because she is too damaged to learn from these other "more successful" (in her scale of success) women, she will hate them, because she is jealous of them. But because woman under patriarchy's first response to another woman who has done what she has failed to do is to hate her for it, so are we duping ourselves. We must dump our egos fast and learn to surrender our bodies and hearts to knowledge, even when it comes from a woman. Not just a woman as a holy mother figure either. But a woman as a sexual being, a woman in all her sensuality and wildness.

You don't only have to take my word for it. A new generation of mothers are thankfully demanding the right to full awareness of one of woman's greatest experiences. There I was sitting, thinking about it prior to writing this, when the phone rang. I went to answer it. It was D. to tell me of her son's birth yesterday. "Intense, inspiring. It's awesome, the power of the birthing force," she said.

"I didn't have to do anything, except surrender to it and go with it, where it took me. All that business about pushing that you are taught is unecessary. Your body does the work. You just concentrate and allow it to happen. Just breathe.

Mindful mastery of the breath. Don't waste any energy. Thank you, a thousand times, for the herbs you gave me, because they made the process so efficient and intense. My uterus contracted so quickly, and I hardly lost any blood." I thanked her for proving it. For sticking out against so many odds and having the birth she wanted.

The need for physical preparation to birth a child.

In the first place, pregnancy is a natural, albeit, occasional, function of a woman's body. It is a great feat, as great a warriors task as leading an army to victory and it deserves as much admiration.

Childbirth without preparation is like taking a driving test without lessons, a matter of luck, rather than wisdom. This is why a woman's body, her vehicle for bringing new life into the world, needs attention.

In order to be healthy and happy, a pregnant woman can do Yoga and meditation, breathe and eat correctly and allow herself relaxation and pleasure. This is doubly so during pregnancy when she has the responsibility of bringing a new soul onto Earth. What an exciting prospect! What a prime time to learn how to nurture, starting with oneself.

The best time to start preparing for a joyful, problem-free pregnancy is ideally before intending to conceive. In practice however, many women do not consciously conceive, and so it may take the stimulus of a confirmed pregnancy to make her decide to "get her act together", as far as her and her baby's health is concerned. But healthy babies start from conception, with healthy parents. So it is advantageous if both the mother and father prepare their physical and emotional health before they conceive.

So much burden is placed on the mother's head as regards the health of her unborn child, whilst the father is often tolerated to behave as a complete slob as far as his health is concerned. Research has shown however that if the father-to-be is in a healthy condition and that if his reproductive organs, powered by his kidneys, are functioning strongly, then his seed for conception will be constitutionally stronger. Healthier fathers and mothers are going to make healthier babies. Both parents can do a lot to tone up and strengthen their reproductive systems by taking herbs, in the form of teas, as early as possible before conceiving.

Certainly as soon as a woman is pregnant she should begin to drink herbal teas on a regular basis. There are many good books on the subject. My experience of using herbs wisely in pregnancy has been borne out by the exceptional results I have seen in terms of the efficiency and uncomplicatedness of the birth process. A mother to be should take not only herbs for the birth, but also those herbs that are vitamin and mineral-rich, and will help to grow a healthy baby.

Most medical practitioners recognise the need for optimum nutrition in pregnancy, but what they have not yet acknowledged is that it makes a difference to the body whether these nutrients are in organic or synthetic form. Vitamins and minerals contained in foods and herbs are the safest and most readily assimilable sources of nutrition. Vitamins and minerals synthesised in a laboratory, or even taken from unusual animal or other sources, do not feed the body in the same way as do vigorous, healthy plants. They do not promote immunity from disease as effectively and the body does not recognise them as healing foods.

Red Raspberry leaf builds the quality of the blood of both mother and baby. It is astringent and mildly contractive for the uterine area. There is however often some confusion among mothers-to-be and their relatives, that this herb can cause miscarriage if taken too early. I will discuss this subject in more detail shortly, however suffice to say that Raspberry leaf will not of itself cause contractions leading to miscarriage. There would have to be other extenuating circumstances. Moreover, my experience of this herb is that it is more therapeutic in pregnancy than words can do justice to. However it should be taken in combination with other nutritional herbs, such as Nettles, Alfalfa and Red Clover, and after the sixth month Squaw Vine, which "allows a woman to give birth with the ease of a wild vixen". (J.De Bairacli Levy).

Raspberry leaf's other attributes are that it tones and strengthens the muscles of the womb and pelvis, thereby relieving muscular and dragging pains in pregnancy, as well as labour and after-birth pains. It also eases morning sickness, thought to be caused by the body not having got used to the high level of hormones, especially progesterone, circulating in the bloodstream in the early stages of the pregnancy. I personally feel that the nausea is also the result of toxicity in the system, particularly the liver, which seems more to store toxicity rather than pass it into the baby's bloodstream.

This is why particular attention should be paid to what a woman eats when she is pregnant. There is an imbecilic fostering of the idea on television that pregnant women will want to eat tuna and banana pizzas, or chocolate and mayonnaise sandwiches, or so the adverts depict us. Cravings for things that are extraordinary are very often nutritional deficiencies that will be further disturbed by the intake of apparently satisfying, but extremely poisonous foods - such as ice cream and sugary snacks, or very salty or fatty foods.

The best thing is to seek a dietary balance and to eat whole grains and vegetables and other foods mainly from plant, rather than animal sources. Then there will be none of the risks of coming into contact with one of the deadly food bugs, like Listeria and Salmonella, that have been made so much the worry of mothers-to-be. If meat and fish are felt to be necessary foods for the woman - there can be no prescribed rules of eating, everyone is different - then it should be organic, free-range and only eaten according to need and not to greed.

Kelp and watercress are two herbs that regulate pituitary gland hormones. Both are also good nutritional sources. Kelp contains iodine, to help normal thyroid function. It also contains zinc, bromium and silica as well as vitamins A, B, (including B 12) C, D and E. Watercress is high in natural iron. It is anti-anaemic and builds the red blood cells. Its constituents also include natural sources of vitamins A, C and D, calcium, iodine, chlorine, fluorine, phosphorus, potassium, sodium, magnesium, iron, manganese, germanium, sulphur, silica, arsenic, niacin, zinc and copper, which are all needed to promote and build immunity from disease in the newborn. In fact kelp and watercress are really superfoods that should be taken throughout pregnancy and lactation. Artificial iron supplements on the other hand, are constipating, often already a problem in pregnancy, and cannot be tolerated by the digestive system. The point is that if foods high in iron content are selected, there will be no need for iron supplementation and there will be less likelihood of blood related disorders such as anaemia and haemorrhage. Nettles, that hated garden weed, are a most valuable source of iron, chlorophyll and other trace elements. They contain lots of vitamin C, B, beta-carotene and up to 24%protein. They replenish deficiency and restore the blood, promote lactation, cleanse the kidneys and are a tonic for the hair. The gardener's enemy is woman's best friend. Or one of them! There are lots of lovely herbs that can be enjoyed during this sacred time.

Plants which should be avoided in pregnancy.

Of the few that should be avoided during pregnancy, they are mainly those strong plants that the nose and taste of a pregnant woman would anyway, naturally steer clear of. However to list contra-indicated herbs, they are; Autumn Crocus, Barberry, Golden Seal, Juniper, Male Fern, Mandrake, Pennyroyal, Poke root, Rue, Sage, Southernwood, Tansy, Thuja and Wormwood. These herbs are stimulating to the uterus and are reputed to trigger abortion or miscarriage. (More about this later).

Pregnancy can be a time of great joy. It depends upon the way it is viewed. It almost always comes as a shock to discover you are pregnant. Once the tester has actually gone pink or blue and confirmed what you may already have known in your body, you are left with a million different things to consider.

Whatever your emotional fluctuations, the main thing to get back to is the truth. You and a soul have connected. This soul has chosen you to bring it through to physical life. This is a special and very spiritual task, in which a woman is deeply bound to the creative will. Whatever the initial fears and constraints, everything will eventually fall into place, given half-a chance. There is no need to suffer. There is never any need to suffer, to put oneself through hell, because there appears to be no other choice. There is always the choice not to suffer, but to accept and embrace life.

This is not to say that abortion is wrong. I do not pass judgement, and neither has anyone else the right to do so. At the end of the day the decision to support growing life must rest with the mother. Any society or group which allocates itself the right to decide for women, is not based so much on baby loving, as on woman-hating. Such a group dares to command the right to enter a woman's body and emotional space, and seeks to influence her personal karma, which only she can create or change. Abortion is a fact of life under patriarchy, where mothers, and sometimes fathers, are left, without community, without love and support, and without the material resources to bring up children. If a woman hasn't got the maturity to cope with an "unwanted" child, the chances are there is no one in her immediate network who can either offer the love that is needed. Sometimes abortion is the preferential option!

Nevertheless, there is no escaping the fact that abortion is an act of butchery, where a foetus is as savagely dragged from the safety of its mother's womb sanctuary, as a lamb is plucked from its hillside. Life, in its prime is suddenly cut off. Abortion is an act against women, as much as it is against children, and feminists should not fall into the trap of thinking that the right to abortion is woman's victory. It is more proof of the masculine scientific progress and control over the reproductive system of victim women. What is a feminist issue is the acceptance and embracing of life, where it did not originally seem to be possible. This is women's victory!

I sometimes get calls from women asking me about the possibility of a herbal abortion. There is this idea that by taking herbs, the issue could be made less complex and it would not be so painful physically, and especially emotionally. My feeling is that a herbal abortion could be even more traumatic than a medical one. A herbal abortion is so unpredictable. You may be waiting for it to happen and it doesn't, which can be very nerve wracking. The only time when it may be worth a try, is when a woman has definitely decided to abort anyway. The good thing about using herbs is that if the attempt fails, it is unlikely to damage the baby, as the purpose of abortion herbs is to make the uterus contract very strongly, and thus deposit its contents, not to kill the baby! However it may cause difficulties later on, if the woman decides to reverse her decision, such as low implantation of the placenta or premature birth. In order to provoke an abortion in a physically healthy pregnancy, the dosage of abortion herbs needs to be very strong indeed and is therefore likely to be irritating to the reproductive organs and body.

It is nature's design to implant and grow a foetus, and in order to prevent this grand plan, one has to challenge nature. It isn't that easy and it may have catastrophic consequences. I am not passing judgement at all. A herbal abortion just isn't a viable alternative for most women. Even if you can get hold of the appropriate herbs, and you do succeed in bringing on an abortion, you may not be able to staunch the bleeding and may need further herbs to do so. Besides which, a herbal abortion carried out without the support of an experienced herbalist could be a very frightening experience.

For some women, considering or even attempting a herbal abortion is anyway only a half decision to abort their babies. They feel that by taking herbs, it will not be so bad. I feel it is more emotionally sound to confront the issue honestly and decide clearly whether or not to have the baby. If you really want to abort, then it is better to go to a clinic and get it over with. But if you don't want to lose your baby then don't mess with herbs. On the other hand if you later decide you will have the baby and a failed herbal abortion attempt is your only way to come to terms with this, as was my own experience with my third child, then the chances are your baby will be fine and just damn glad to be here after all!

Herbs are the Earth's first line of children. They contain her essence and life force. Their purpose is to sustain and nourish life, rather than to destroy it. They are agents of God's will. When herbs are used for a specific purpose they may just do the opposite. Last year a woman in the middle of a miscarriage rang me for help. She had been bleeding for some time and wanted to complete the miscarriage. She had not wanted the baby, but neither was she able to let go of it physically or psychically. She was caught in the middle ground between acceptance and rejection. I gave her a herbal formula specifically recommended to complete a miscarriage. I sent her home with instructions to make and drink the tea, and to prepare to let go of the baby. I expected she would lose the baby within the next few days. In actual fact, the herbs stopped the bleeding and sealed up the pregnancy. She decided that she was really pleased after all, and in the end, thankful that she did not lose the baby, delivered a bouncing baby boy a few months later. There are many stories about herbs like this. They are the mistresses of spiritual miracles, and woman's true allies.

Many women cannot accept the responsibility of of giving birth to and nurturing another human being. It may be a natural thing for a woman to do, but this does not necessarily equip her to deal with the non-biological functions of motherhood. Some women have been too hurt themselves, by their own frightened mothers, to be able to be adult enough to have a baby of their own. They are suffering the developmental arrest of the abandoned child. Such a resistance to motherhood can give rise to physical complications in the pregnancy and delivery, as well as profoundly affect the child, who will likely also experience the rejection vibe. Sometimes however, having a baby of your own can break this pattern and make you whole. It can heal a damaged childhood, bring back the child spirit spark of joy. A child can be the fun that you were never allowed to have.

Pregnancy too can be fun. It is important to make every moment of your pregnancy as aware as possible. Because relatively, being pregnant occupies such a short time in a woman's life, and it is a good reason to give yourself permission to let go, to relax, to go deep into bliss and joy, and to dump struggle. As Stuart Wilde, the healer, points out, effort is one thing, but struggle is quite another. Struggle involves effort plus negative emotion, which debilitates and decreases life force. As Stuart says in the title of one of his little pocket guides, "Life was never meant to be a struggle!"

It is crazy to rush around in pregnancy, as so many women do, trying to prove they are Superwoman, hell-bent on showing that their pregnancy isn't affecting them. It's part of the "cover-up syndrome", that is rather a patriarchal reversal, in the sense that we deny and diminish our woman-ly differences. Just as many of us were brought up to call our periods "the curse", and to view them as some kind of inter-ruption to real life, so there is still a tendency to view preg-nancy as some kind of onerous burden which excludes us from participation in normal life. Some of us just put on our slippers and start to shuffle around. Perhaps this is because in patriarchy pregnancy and sexuality are seen as so incom-patible. Strange when you think how babies are made! Models who have proudly exposed their swollen bellies have been greeted with cries of, "cover it up, no one wants to see your bump". This negation of woman's sexuality while pregnant obviously hurts the female ego, which depends upon sexual strokes for its fuel. The resultant competition for mum's body that occurs, between society (men) and the baby, is obscene and is perhaps one reason why so few women do actually breast-feed. At the moment it seems, society is win-ning the competition for the psychic ownership of woman's body, with the baby coming strongly second. It would appear almost as if some women have babies just to put them in prams and cots just as soon as they are born, so detached from their own flesh and blood they have permitted them-selves to become.

It is these women's loss, poor souls, and it is important not to get angry with them. It is so beautiful to be pregnant. One can go into a space of dreams and rest, connecting with the growing baby inside your belly - talking to him, healing her and passing your love feelings through. For these few months, pregnancy is so short, it is time to forget the banality of "Monday morning life".

Even if you still want or have to work, unless you are fortunate enough to have your own business or do some-thing you truly love, know that it is just a means to an end. It is not spiritually important, not like the baby, don't let it drain you. Just keep your mind fixed on the handiwork of the divine - that growing spark of life within you that is the co-operation of you and your partner and God - your baby. Because the baby is untainted with the heaviness of life and is pure. Therefore your baby is your spiritual teacher. She or he has come to show you a little bit of heaven, and your challenge is not to impose the negativity of your own experience on to him or her - your medicine baby,- but to let them develop as they will, whilst you guide. That is what motherhood is, the guidance of the unborn and later, the child.

As I said, you can really help yourself and your unborn baby with the correct use of herbs for pregnancy and childbirth. Wise women and midwives have always known about them and thank heavens they still do. There are many good books that go into depth on the subject. My favourite one currently is "The Wise Woman Herbal for the Childbearing Year", by Susun Weed. Some women worry about using herbs in pregnancy, believing that they may cause miscarriage. Let me emphasise something here about the use of herbs in pregnancy and in general. Pregnancy herbs will not cause miscarriage or any other trauma of pregnancy. Herbs always work to support the body in its healing process. Sometimes however, our bodies are in such a weakened or debilitated state that they simply cannot withstand a pregnancy and birth. The herbs may prompt the body to do what is the most energy efficient thing - in other words to dump its load. In this sense miscarriage is beneficial, because it allows a woman a second chance to clean up her act, so to speak, and get herself more prepared physically to carry a baby in future.

Miscarriage can occur because of physical weakness, exhaustion and unpreparedness. But it can also happen because the mother's will is not engaged in her pregnancy. She may not even be aware of this. The baby's will too may be a factor. Some souls decide to cop out after all, despite an initial decision to incarnate for whatever reason. Such happenings totally defy all rational explanation, a factor which doctors often find extremely aggravating and unacceptable, as they doggedly battle to gain a scientific directory of women's reproductive activity.

Reproductive technologies are among the most potentially lethal interventions into nature, that are likely to end up with such mutational and laboratory type results, that they are very damaging to the health and balance of the earth. Infertility treatment, with all its ramifications, is one such area of reproductive technology that needs to be considered. I am not against technology where it is used to free peoples' spirits from suffering. A female developed and designed technology is called for, which is intent only on addressing need, but not on playing the hero and attempting to free humanity from the 'constraints' and limitations of nature. What these scientists have failed to realise as they play power-dangling gods over vulnerable peoples' lives, is that nature is infinitely more sophisticated than they. There is a wisdom and intelligence in nature, as well as a built- in safety factor, that simply does not occur in the laboratory. This is because the quest for human glory is at the root of reproductive technology, and not, despite what you might think, the plight of childless women. That is only the fuel. The real driving force of such scientific research and development is the ego victory kick of boldly going where no man has gone before.

Many, many women find it offensive and dangerous that science has taken their reproductive power and assumed the right to manipulate and control it, beyond the point where it has been required, by women, to go. The results of such experimentation are unpredictable, the consequences often far worse than the woman's acceptance of her body's initial inability to conceive.

We now have sixty year old mothers, surrogate mothers, babies conceived out of ovaries made from the cells of aborted foetuses, babies conceived outside the womb in test-tubes, by people in white coats. There are babies kept alive inside brain dead or comatose mothers. Women so desperate to become mothers that they will spend years undergoing painful tests and treatments to further damage their reproductive systems. They may deny the earthly pleasures of sex with their partner in preference for artificial insemination, which might be more 'scientific' for fertility. We now have previously infertile women having multiple births. A woman who wanted a baby ended up with six (sextuplets); they all died. Women who were treated with growth hormone from infected corpses in the 1950's must now wait to see if they have developed BSE (Mad cow disease).

Science has finally made what it calls a breakthrough on sex selection. Not only can farmers now get the correct ratio of milk to beef, but parents can finally choose the sex of their babies. It need no longer be left to nature to create the ratio of male to female children, but to human, cultural preference. As we know, given the choice, many cultures and religions would not want girls, and in their attempt to control and deny nature they will disrupt the balance of humanity. But worse than this, because the former's is the crime of ignorance, are the scientists who have participated in these so-called breakthroughs. We will be left with endless debates about ethics, and it is to be hoped that the wisdom and maturity of those who will decide, prevails. If we reject such intervention as immoral, will not the development of such technologies have been a costly time-wasting exercise?

Childbirth is NOT a medical prerogative.

The problem as I see it, is that we are already in the mould of intervention into women's reproductive lives. The moment a woman becomes pregnant, she is obliged to notify the medical authorities who will manage her pregnancy and birth for her. There is an issue of feminist ethics here. It concerns the theft of women's reproductive power. The point is that at all levels, there is an implicit assumption, that women, although they are the bearers of children, most certainly do not possess the rights to control over anything concerned with their creation, birth or rearing.

In other words, we are seen, not as the servants of God, but as the servants of the patriarchal regime, that expects us to breed children, not for our own pleasure and happiness, but for the perpetuation of its own needs and ideologies. I, for one simply do not find it acceptable to surrender my body's wisdom and secrets to an ant-like process devoid of love and compassion. But at this present time in our history we really have no choice. It is an issue of the upmost urgency that mothers reclaim maternity from the domain of medicine. The reason why so many women experience such difficulty in giving birth is because we surrender our own power and responsibility in the process to patriarchal expectations.

Drained and depressed by the battle, before it has even begun, we allow ourselves to give way. The vulnerability and sensitivity of an isolated pregnant or birthing woman is a fact. We feel we are no match for the mighty might of the militaristic establishment that calls us to account. Let me assure you now of the real truth, that there is no match for the mighty might of a happily and naturally birthing woman. That is an awesome force! It is our right to non-medical childbirth. It is our claim. Childbirth is ours and ours alone to do what we want with. It is a family affair under the mother's jurisdiction. If she wishes to share it then so be it. What we will not be made to do, is to accept others expectations and definitions of our experience.

And we most certainly will not permit these precious,

joyous, once-in-a-lifetime, life experiences to be taken over by so called professionals. There is only one professional in the matter of having a baby, and that is the mother herself! If she asks for help, that's a different matter. Those who work in the area of childbirth, midwives and doctors, are serving God. It is truly divine work. They are not serving themselves and they would do as well to remember that, before the day of reckoning, when mothers will control childbirth, arrives.

The problem for us lies in developing enough confidence in ourselves to "go it alone" and wrench back our power to command our own birth experiences. This is not to say that we should approach maternity unsupported. Far from it. I believe that we should have as much emotional and physical support as we need. This however is different from the social and legal expectation that we consult professionals in the matter of our pregnancies. It is presently absolutely taken for granted and I might add almost universally accepted, that a woman is doing the best for herself and her unborn baby, by submitting to regular routine ante-natal care. If a woman is uneducated and unconfident about pregnancy and birth, advice and support are crucial to her well-being, but the emphasis of all current childbirth practice today, is on the pregnant woman as an obstetric object. All ante-natal, natal and post-natal routine views the woman in terms of the condition and functionability of her perineum. A pregnant woman is, to the medical professionals, no more than a walking belly, whose reproductive organs become the area of close scrutiny and measurability. Midwives may have a better bedside manner than doctors, but it does not deny the fact that they are still carrying out 'doctor's orders', in terms of the policies they are obliged to adopt.

Midwives are always in danger of being "struck-off", since caring behaviour might breach health authority rules. Most prefer to play safe, even at the mother's discomfort.

The point is that medical policy is not "mother-centred, it is administration-centred, and like all hierarchical organisations exists to serve itself. Mothers-to-be as the recipients of medical care, must fit into the same framework as patients, who are often helpless in terms of their decision-making capacities. The general assumption that pregnant women require the involvement of health service professionals prevents the rise of woman-centred birth, because woman-centred health is individualistic, viewing each woman as a unique being with unique needs, and natural, using appropriate health methods and medicines that do not cause harm to any level of life in the process. The application of mass policies to women, on either a national or even a local health-authority level, cannot but have serious consequences for any who do not fit into the rigid policy. Since policies are not conceived on the level of compassion, because compassion is about using the heart as the gauge, they cannot be acceptable to women giving birth, where sensitivity and adaptability to the situation are the necessary keys. There are so many examples of sensitive midwives being "struck-off" midwives, or nearly so, that it serves to act as a warning for any midwife, or less so, doctor, acting appropriately, rather than prescribedly. Small wonder that so many midwives leave the service in frustration, while others carry on with averted eyes. Neither category of isolated frightened mouse is yet able to provoke change by confronting the issue, which is that childbirth is not a medical imperative. Choice within birth is not the issue here. It is choice about birth, that is at stake.

That choice is whether or not to involve the medical profession in one's own life events, and the freedom not to do so without penalty. I believe every woman must have the right to enjoy pregnancy without medical involvement or notification. She alone is entitled to request ante-natal or post-natal care, or alternatively to make her own non-medical arrangements, without judgement or fear of persecution, for either herself or her helpers. Mothers-to-be should not have to refuse medical care either, it is a question of it being available on request for those who are not yet ready or willing to take responsibility for themselves and their children, whilst those who want to do so are left alone.

My personal view involves the total rejection of what is currently agreed ante-natal and post-natal practice, including all routine blood and urine testing, weighing, blood pressure taking, and electronic foetal monitoring. This also includes the more injurious post-natal practices such as Guthrie tests, heel pricking, vitamin injection and phototherapy as well as the refusal of mothers to be physically separated from their babies at any stage against their wills, from the simplest removals, such as for bathing or weighing, to the long-term separations involved in neo-natal incubation. It is an extreme offence against women to build neo-natal units where mothers cannot also make their temporary homes alongside their infants and participate equally in their care. It is based on an assumption that the disadvantaged premature baby needs medical care first and foremost, before it needs its mother, to say nothing of the mother, who has been prematurely robbed of her pregnancy, and her healing needs.

Mothers need also expect the right not to be judged or categorised as likely to put their own unborn babies at risk, and all of us need to refuse to admit to being a risk to our own children by any of our free will choices. We will not accept the assumption of any one, health professional or relative, that they can come between the primary bond of mother and baby in either thought, word or deed. The medical profession must relinquish the right to be outraged on behalf of our babies, and at our choices not to involve them in our experience, and they must cease to consider themselves central to it. True compassion is allowing a woman to take responsibility for her decisions and actions, and relinquishing the right to make judgements and apportion blame.

Ecstatica

The time has come to awaken to the fact that the right to control one among our most special and moving life experiences has been stolen from us. That is the experience of childbirth. We are now obliged to fight for the right to full awareness of our own experience, so ridden with intervention is it! By putting a precedent on birth as a medical and bureaucratic matter, patriarchy has robbed us of our domain, and our definition of childbirth. By continuing to allow this to occur, in spite of the opposition we face, we are depriving ourselves of our healing and hence our power. By accepting the birth of our children as medical matters, once we become conscious of what is going on, we are surrendering ourselves to an unrespectful authority, intent on playing god. But because it is a power that puts its own heroic needs first, it is at the expense of our own joy and ecstasy.

Pregnancy and birth is the ultimate love experience. It is a time when a woman is most closely connected to her divinity. Particularly during those few hours she is giving birth, she needs deep concentration on her labouring body's rhythms. She can choose to go into a totally "silent", i.e. beyond mental thought, space.

Therefore anyone who comes along to interrupt that state of being for their own needs, or the needs of a system such as bureaucratic or administrative needs, is committing a hugely disrespectful act. This is so even when this action is supposedly for the benefit of the mother herself, for example vaginal examinations, foetal monitoring and so forth, because even such small interruptions can cause the progress of labour to be disrupted and thus alter the whole course and nature of the experience and also possibly even affect the ultimate outcome. Such interruptions of her rhythmic flow allow and encourage doubt to enter the mind, and as we all know, thought predetermines reality. A fleeting moment of anxiety, a shadow of doubt, could under some circumstances, gain enough momentum to turn a labour into a nightmare experience. Despite health authorities best attempts to disguise modern labour rooms, with patterned wallpapers, double beds, bean bags, rocking cribs and even birth pools, nothing, absolutely nothing, can change the intention behind the set-up, which is the arrogant and woman-mistrusting philosophy, that hospitals are the correct and safest places for women to give birth in. Women should not be fooled into thinking that because a room has been made to look homely, it is therefore as good as a home-birth. If the authorities really believed we were better off giving birth at home, they wouldn't send us to hospital to have our babies. By doing up the delivery rooms, they are stealing the idea of the comfort and relaxedness of a home-birth, which can truly only occur at home.

Only mothers give birth. No-one else. The people present at the birth, those assisting her, can share the experience, but they must not attempt to control it. Anyone entering a birthing room should be prepared to leave the contents of their heads at the door. This includes their pre-judgements about the mother and her capacity to give birth and above all their anxieties, conscious or not, about birth itself.

Birth is primarily a woman's event, at which selected men may be invited to participate. These men may be the babies fathers, the mother's partners, friends or relatives, but the point is they should only be there because she loves and trusts them. No other men have any right to interfere in, or with, a woman's birth.

Should the need for support arise, it should not be viewed as intervention. If obstetricians were all servants of women, as they must eventually become, then we would expect more respectful treatment of a woman's body. Pregnancy is pregnancy and labour is labour. The present policy of separating births into levels of normality and abnormality is divisive of women, and leads to feelings of failure and inadequacy on the part of those women who have had to undergo obstetric intervention.

Ecstatica

We are going to have to work hard to dismiss the entrenched notion of birth as a fearful event. As more of us reclaim our right to experience the birth we choose, albeit with the authorities resistance, so the success stories will start to overtake the horror ones. We need to ensure an absolute dismissal of the idea that birth is something to be feared. A categoric rejection of birth portrayed as suffering in art and culture. It is this deeply-rooted fear, activated in us in pregnancy, that makes us permit our pregnancies and births to be medicalised. Deep inside every one of us is a voice, however faint, that asks, "What if something goes wrong? "

What should go wrong? There is only one thing that can go wrong, and that is our own brains. Our minds control the nature of our experience. They have the power to make it good or make it bad, or just to go on vacation and leave someone else to handle the experience however they see fit. This is what we do. We do not enjoy full awareness while being pregnant or giving birth, because we are not "permitted" to by the countless interruptions to our "meditation" that the maternity system demands.

From the very first emotional exhilaration point of realising we are pregnant, the free flow of our experience is undercut by conditions and constraints. We are required to notify the relevant medical authority; hospital, doctor, midwife, as soon as we discover our new state. In some cases it is even they who inform us we are pregnant! (At least it always is in TV soaps). In so doing we are also yielding the responsibility of pregnancy to professional agencies, outside of ourselves. There is no way out of this as yet without penalty. In the event that we do not register for ante-natal care, simply because we do not choose to, because we feel great and confident in our own bodies ability to be natural, we are likely to be reported to punitive authorities, and categorised by welfare workers as putting our own babies, growing inside our own bodies, at risk.

This is the most outrageously insulting approach to women, mothers-to-be, who are being psychologically, and often ultimately physically, separated from their babies, through another's subjective judgement of their behaviour. No one should presume the right to come between a mother and her baby. No matter what the circumstances are, none should dare to break the bond, even in thought.

The bond that exists between mother and baby is the most sacred connection on this planet. Death cannot break it even. It is not something we have to learn, although social pressures can weaken and damage it, it just happens by divine will. It is part of the "big plan". In its face, all shall remain humble, and allow it to be the healing force that it is designed to be, that nourishes not only the baby, but the whole planet. As mother Earth protects her "children", i.e. all life, night and day, so a human mother protects her baby. For anyone to assume or decide this is not the case is a violation of human freedom, and therefore a karmic offence.

It is true that there are some mothers who are less than naturals. Mothers who are "sick" and who, in bringing children into the world, may expose them to suffering. But the systematic battering of the mother, the reinforcement of her negativity and the reminders of her inadequacies, will neither do anything to help her to overcome her limitations. She and her child will simply become sicker and sicker as the bond between them is interfered with and eroded. There is also the often overlooked possibility that, left to her own experience, the baby will afford her healing opportunities, with the result that both lives will become enriched and changed for the better.

But the common, authoritarian, "naughty-girl" stance is punitive, rather than constructive, and it defers shame rather than healing. In fact when approached by health professionals with this attitude, a resistant mother is not going to be afforded healing opportunity, unless in the end she gets so wild and angry that she gets her act together. (I mean as a woman warrior!)

No one in the health, social or bureaucratic authority has the right to categorise a mother, or interfere with her natural right to bear a child in freedom and with self-definition. This applies across the board to all mothers.

Not only does no one have the right to confer judgement. Neither does the medical profession have the right to categorise a mother in medical jargon. Terms like primips and multigravida(medical descriptions of the number of pregnancies and births we have had)are disrespectful and de-humanising. We are women and we are mothers. But we are not medical terms! The insulting predisposition of medicine to view us as mechanical models, no more than the sum of our parts, is bound to lead to suffering for those who do not fit within that framework. The notes that are made on us throughout pregnancy and birth see us in terms of the condition of our cervixes and our breasts, the quality and quantity of our urine, our blood pressures and blood losses. Nowhere is it written that we are people, and it is not our pelvises, but our thoughts and emotions that predominantly define our birth experience. Therefore we must absolutely reject any such descriptions of us according to medical terminology.

Even less does someone have the right to enter our homes and to attempt to influence us according to their own beliefs about birth. The notion of informed choice in birth matters, offered by midwives and doctors, is inapplicable, because a mother's choices are not informed, so long as they are presented by midwives in their function as medical agents, on behalf of and paid by the health service. They are therefore ultimately more responsible to the health service hierarchy than the woman. Besides this, if someone comes into our home in a uniform, while we are in our nighties, they can hardly be said to be representing choice of any sort. What they are representing is a belief system about birth and life in general, in which the implicit inequalities, despite their own personal levels of education or compassion, make it difficult for them to accept a woman's opinion as knowledge, or her right to self-diagnosis, despite her obvious intelligence. Our point of view is therefore deemed "unscientific", since they are the health professionals. We, the mothers, become the recipients of their professional expertise. That is presumption, not informed choice!

The starting point of any such choice must anyway be the woman at the centre of her pregnancy as well as the directress of it. Home birth is the obvious option of where to give birth. But a woman must have the right to bear a child in whatever position, location or environment she feels comfortable in, with qualified and loving support available to her should she require it. Not if she doesn't.

Whilst home birth is just about becoming a recognised and long-fought for right, non-medical birth is not. Mothers who want a non-medical birth cannot have one, without fear of being persecuted and prosecuted. We urgently need more truly independent, woman-centred midwives, accountable to none but themselves, the woman they are attending and God. The nearest a mother can get to this ideal today is to pay a private, independent, but health authority and national nursing board trained and accountable, midwife, to support her in her adult choices and to negotiate the minefield between health authority and naturally birthing mother. I'm not saying there aren't some wonderful community and hospital midwives around,there are. But privacy affords some degree of protection to the mother-to-be, and if there is any possibility of affording to pay one of these midwives, it may be worth it for their commitment to her. However it should not have to be this way! Mothers also need to be committed to protective midwives, as these women are more likely to attract criticism for their liberal and trusting treatment of the birthing woman. It is interesting to note that the word midwife derives from German and means literally "with woman".

Midwives are caught in the middle of the minefield between mothers and the authorities, trying not to get blown up. The bureaucracy and dominance attitude that surrounds their practice, in the form of paperwork and legality, renders them powerless to truly protect a woman according to her requests. The midwife has to satisfy the authorities and the authorities could not give a monkey's uncle about the emotional and spiritual quality of birth. If women conform, it is a lot easier to operate a smooth system. Hospital affords the perfect opportunity to control them. Home is further beyond their jurisdiction. So is a birth pool, the sea, under a bush or anywhere else a woman might choose to give birth. Small wonder that so many babies seem to get born before the midwife could get there, or other such surprises. Such women are lucky enough to defy the hugely long note-taking process, that goes on record for at least a part, perhaps the most intense part, of the pregnancy. For even the most radical of midwives is still duty bound to make copious records, arming herself with a mountain of paperwork about the woman, as if she were a statistic, so dangerous has her job become. She may be sued for malpractice by the mother at any time within the next 25 years. Conscious of this aspect, it takes a humble midwife indeed to approach the mother in an attitude of trust and respect.

However benevolently her approach is carried out, it still has the effect of pressuring a woman to conform (or rebel) to others expectations. Most midwives in this country are expected to wear a utilitarian uniform. There is no escaping the separation that is artificially imposed by this system of maternity between mothers and midwives. The wearing of nurses uniforms emphasises midwives' official status over mothers, primarily encouraging them to bury their sisterhood and woman empathies. They can then nicely fulfil the status of "token torturers" of women on behalf of the patriarchy. It further reminds us that most midwives in this country started off their training with an intention to nurse sick people. A midwife practicing today may have spent years training in the routines of bedpans and blood-tests. She may genuinely want ultimately to become a midwife, or she may only see it as another department of healthcare. Even though she may approach the woman in an attitude of service, it is prescriptive service. Unless she is very sensitive indeed, and I know there are midwives who are, she may still be controlling the woman's experience, by the requirements she must fulfil in her allegiance to duty.

Midwives must never forget that they are doing divine work. Aiding and educating women in the process of carrying and birthing new life is truly to walk at God's side. To witness these miracles is a privilege. It can also be emotionally draining, painful and stressful. It is only by the grace of divine will that a woman can continue to serve in this way and she needs the discipline and technique to re-create and re-generate her energies to do this work. She also needs support and tender loving care. But above all, she needs to rectify her relationship with God, because if she approaches birth as a divine servant, acting from her intuitive, healer brain with love, she will be blessed. In this way she will be a blameless and fearless midwife despite authoritarian pressure. But she may need to challenge herself to find the humility and respect to permit a woman to birth in her own way, even if she does not agree with it.

Birth is easy when it is approached as a meditation. When it is entered wholeheartedly, as part of the ebb and flow of life, a healthy woman can grow and birth a baby with the flow and dynamism of a Pacific roller. But when her pregnancy is directed and controlled by the requirements of a vast impersonal system, she is not her own mistress, since she is obliged to notify, explain and justify her choices to another. This is when birth can start to go wrong. It is why there are so many "difficult" births. There is this aura of fear surrounding birth at every level of the process. The fear of surrendering to the unknown is for many first time mothers inhibiting, as is the fear of repeating a negative experience for subsequent mothers. The fear of causing ripples and even losing their jobs may cause midwives to stand in opposition against the woman, at the cost of their instincts. Hang in there and ride the roller coaster.

Chapter 2.
Tantric Birth, Rapture and Post-Natal Retreat.

The breath is the key to healing birth. A birthing woman needs complete concentration on her task. She also needs to summon up her full power, by mindful mastery of her breath. By this I mean breathing from her belly, using the breath as a motor force to power the body and to propel the baby on its journey downward. The exhalation is extremely important, because the better and more strongly a woman can exhale , the more she can let go, and efficient birth is about the ability to let go completely, even when there is pain. Since it is not the pain of illness, it need not be feared, and therefore the trick is to open oneself as fully and gladly as possible, despite the discomfort. This is not hard, but it does require preparation, and this is why Yoga and Meditation in pregnancy classes exist, and what they specifically need to address.

Sexual inhibitedness makes it very difficult for a woman to let go to give birth to her child. There can be a lot of difficulty surrendering to the force of the birth, in being totally receptive and open to the birthing energy, which sweeps a woman along with it, unless she resists. There is nothing more asexual, more sterile and unemotional, than having strange men in white coats present and watching.

Because the nature of birth is earthy, lusty and wild. It is rude and uncomformist. It makes you groan and moan and writhe and sweat. It is in total breach of the normal mildness and politeness that is expected of women. No wonder it takes a strong woman to defy society in order to obey her nature!

Ecstatica

After the baby has been born and everything has been attended to there is a need for the new mother (and father too) to rest and refresh, as well as a period of adjustment to the effect of a new baby on their lives. I cannot emphasise enough the absolute need for a period of retreat, at least for the mother and baby, which should be no less than forty days. The new family needs healing time and space - mental space in which to rest, dream, pray, give thanks and celebrate new life. The mother is aided in this spiritual work by the tremendous rapture and bliss that floods in after the birth, during which she will feel as if she is in love again. And she is. She is in love with her baby and in love with the divine force of creation, and this is not something to be squandered.

However it is important for her to remember that most people are not experiencing this height of emotion and have either forgotten or have never experienced it. This is why it is so easy for the new mother to get drained and lose her joy. There can be so much pressure in the family, with domestic needs and chores, from needy relatives and also from health workers, all of whom wish to impose mundane reality onto the new family. This is another way in which the sanctity and sanctuary of birth is stolen from us. By intrusions into the bliss state by those who are not in bliss.

We need to learn how to let nothing come between us and our divine coating that is the prerogative of those who have just given birth. This is why we need and have the right to expect a lengthy period of retreat into which unwelcome people and vibrations may not come. Retreat does not mean that we just lie in bed all day, but it is a period of withdrawal from the mundane, for spiritual awareness and regeneration, which heals. It is also important to protect the new baby from negativity. Obviously relatives are entitled to visit the mother and baby. Health professionals however are not, if they have not been invited. Nevertheless the system assumes that the midwife's and health visitor's services will

84

be required. It is important that these busy professionals develop the sensitivity to walk into the home of the new mother with the humility to allow ecstatic consciousness to prevail. They should be prepared to psychically disrobe themselves and enter into the state of prayer and devotion of the household.

For the mother, it is more a question of being aware of the subtlety of the time and having the confidence to refuse to allow unecessary interruption to her retreat. Birth is sacred. To interrupt the mother's retreat to fulfil one's own needs is an act against God and very karmic.

A mother who does not value herself highly will not allow herself time to go into the depths of her soul with her new infant. Instead of enjoying the bonding and fusing in love with her new baby, she will deny or cut short this imperative. So many mothers are already thinking about going back to work, even before the baby is born, that all emotion is lived to a timetable. This is the way we live today and it is very damaging and makes us hard and cut-off from our children and ourselves.

There is just not enough nurturing support available for mothers in the isolated, nuclear way we live today. Sometimes there is a Grandma around. But there is rarely a community of spiritual support for the mother. New babies are given presents. The cards usually show the baby as a bundle of joy. There is scarcely any celebration of new motherhood. But motherhood is all about change. It represents transition to a new role. Each birth has been the traversing of a shamanic journey close to the edges of life and death. American Indians consider that during birth a woman has gone down to retrieve a new soul.

But in our culture these changes are not honoured. There is no marker of respect. We do not have any rituals to honour our new mothers who have completed a warriors task in bringing new life through. Far from it, a woman suddenly finds herself launched into motherhood, with a crying baby, a growing list of domestic duties and a balancing act, if the family are to cope. Coupled with this there is so much more emphasis on the baby than the mother. The mother Goddess is not a popular icon in contemporary society. Mothers are the unseen forces behind the family, who labour on quietly with the domestic. They are not permitted to indulge in bliss, because they always have to be too busy, and too tired. The pressures on a new mother to "get back to normal" are enormous in our society. A woman in ecstasy just conjures up so much rage in those who need her constant attention and will not permit her to get into her healing, bliss. It is just one of the ways in which woman-hating denial happens in patriarchal societies.

We need to have rituals of support and celebration, whereby a woman who has had a baby is honoured and feted by her friends and relatives. Other women who have had babies could come and give her gifts of food and clothes and help her in whatever way she needs. A new mother needs to be respected as a figure of power and wisdom, who can teach us all of the mystery of life by her recent experience. This seems a far picture from the shuffling, slippered, emotionally drained new mother, who has been denied the knowledge that what she has just experienced is the most natural, consciousness-expanding experience that she is ever likely to have. She is an open channel to the divine. Her body is like a chalice being filled with angelic energy.

Until the day when we are able to accept our own responsibility for the enjoyment of the post-birth state, with its highs and lows, ups and downs, joy and grief and all the profound depth and range of emotions that we can experience, and to understand that it is there for our healing and the healing of the planet, we will have it taken from us by those who do not respect it. If we will not allow ourselves as new mothers to marvel at the awesome splendour of the working of life's mystic law then who else will? Let us not diminish the power of Creation, ourselves, or our children. The post-natal period exists for a spiritual purpose. It is to welcome the soul of the new child. It is for healing the body of the mother and it is to release the grief of separation of the baby's physical entity from its mother's body - this is why the mother is so emotionally fragile.

At the same time, mother and baby are building on this unseen relationship, and learning how to make a physical relationship in the outer world. All this is crucial divine work. Anything which detracts from this as a pull in order to fulfil its own needs, comes second to the primary spiritual and survival functions of the post-natal period, and it can wait. Heaven on the other hand can't, because it won't always be so easily accessible as it is for the short time after the birth.

Make no mistake. This is a long sleep we have had, in which we have switched off from the terror, pain and humiliation we have come to believe earmarks childbirth. We have not been permitted to define our own birth experiences for aeons. Nevertheless it is our contemporary task to reclaim maternity and each do our bit to heal womankind. We will heal ourselves and heal our children, who as babies have been the victims of policy-first birth. More than this we will ensure that never again will we desert our children as they emerge into everyday life, nor will we allow them to be frightened or brutalised by their birth and early experience as we make the choice to heal countless generations of the, as yet, unborn.

CHAPTER 2
Women as Nourishers.

Does anyone know what breasts are for?

A visiting alien might be moved to question why human children appear to be reared on a massive scale by a foster mother of another species. What, they might ask, is so wrong with human mothers that they cannot nourish their own young? Why do cows rear human babies?

Statistics on breast-feeding show that of the mothers who begin to breast-feed their babies, the vast majority have given up by the time their babies are six weeks old. The main reason cited for this is feeling that they don't have enough milk for their babies. Further research decided that this covered the real reason for giving up breast-feeding so soon. When questioned further, a large number of women said they were actually embarrassed about feeding their babies in front of anyone - even relatives. The fact that such a large group of women consider it embarrassing to breast-feed their babies constitutes a major threat to women's physical and emotional health. It highlights the confusion that we have about our own bodies. It is precisely because we feel we do not own our own bodies that we choose to relegate the deepest needs of our infants, as we choose for other animal species to relegate their infants' needs to ours. The whole thing is a ridiculous vicious circle!

Because we are too embarrassed to feed the issue of our bodies, a process which happens automatically in the womb, we take the milk of another species to do it for us. This of course is lethal for our babies, because cows milk is for baby calves who must grow to 1000lbs or so in body weight as soon as possible, and have four stomachs to digest the stuff. It is also pretty bad for us too, because the misuse of our breasts and the fears and phobia that relate around the use of our mammaries, are likely to lead us to all manner of breast diseases and abnormalities. As one of the Hawaiian Kahuna healers seven philosophic principles says, energy flows where attention goes. Conversely obsessive, negative emotion targeted at an area of the body causes build ups and blockages of energy - disease.

I am not saying that not breast-feeding our children will cause breast cancer, because I have not carried out research on the subject. But there are studies to show that there is a very low, almost non-existent rate of breast cancer in cultures where the women exclusively breast-feed.

It is interesting that as a child I remember getting my amusement, with my school friends, from looking at the National Geographic magazines in the school library. We would giggle at the pictures of tribal women with bare breasts!

Little did we realise then that they were in fact accomplishing with ease, a primal and natural function of motherhood that we "sophisticates" in the West find completely baffling. These women provide the knowledge for us that it can be done and it is simple to breast-feed, because they just do it-or at least they did, before the marketing men from the baby milk companies moved in en masse and made them feel that breast-feeding was a low status, last resort. If you are poor and hungry and cannot make enough milk to feed your baby, they will kindly donate powdered infant milk. How much better to give the lactating mother food! But this approach would be the compassionate one, and compassion will not sell products that aren't necessary, and so has no obvious commercial advantage.

Other ways in which Patriarchy has done its work well

in persuading women against breast-feeding, is by depriving women of the opportunity to stay in the nest with their young, due to the economic pressures of having to get back to work as soon as possible, often within six weeks of the birth. This is still within the important post-natal healing period, but in order to safeguard their jobs, and their obviously crucial income, they feel they have no choice. This patriarchal pressure on women - to get back to work - provides an excellent reason against and excuse for not breast-feeding. No sooner has one established feeding one's infant, than one is required to give up feeding and to hand over a bottle weaned infant to a childminder or nursery, and to a tight schedule, rush off to work, where one must spend all or most of the day without one's closest love. This in itself can make breast-feeding a difficult thing to establish and become an unconscious emotional issue, whereby the mother is cutting off the flow of her emotions, as well as her milk, for fear of becoming too attached and then not be able to give up feeding in order to go back to work.

It is absolutely obscene that work places are not designed to bring children to, with flexible start times and creches where mothers can breast-feed on demand. However this does not happen because women are too dependent on the benevolence of employers to provide such facilities. But at the end of the day women need to get together and organise their own. Having your child close to you at work is not a perk-it is an absolute right and prerogative for new mothers who wish to work to be able to combine breast-feeding and working, in the least stressful, most harmonious way.

Personally, I feel nothing can be worth sacrificing the breast-feeding relationship with your baby for. There is a way around every difficult corner. Even if you have to come home at lunchtime or can only feed the baby from when you get home until when you leave the next morning, it is still viable and rewarding to breast-feed. There is nothing like rushing home after a tough day to a waiting, open-mouthed infant who happily latches on to his mum's breast in greeting. Breast-feeding your baby is about much more than just milk. It is about the connection of your baby's mouth to your breast and the love that flows between you, because of this fusion between you. It is a God given opportunity for love. I feel this is the real reason why so many women don't or won't breast-feed, despite the excuses and reasons that are cited for not breast-feeding - such as lack of time, embarrassment, exhaustion, work demands etc. Many mothers are so emotionally blocked that they are incapable of experiencing love, unable to open up to emotional fusion with their babies. Despite what they think are the reasons, the real reason is fear of love and an inability to connect in love with one's own baby. This is not to say that a non-breast-feeding mother cannot experience the same level of connection that a breast-feeding mum can. However the act of breast-feeding serves to remind you of your need to lovingness several times a day. Breast-feeding is an act of devotion, a religious rite, because it requires you to surrender to your baby and to the power of the universe as it manifests in your little miracle from God.

Difficulties experienced in and with breast-feeding, stem from difficulties in accepting and surrendering to motherhood. Indeed selfless service can easily be viewed as a drudge, especially if one has other things on one's mind. On the other hand one can choose to view motherhood as the honour that it truly is and therefore determine not to miss a moment of such a sacred experience. In this way one can accept the tiredness and exhaustion as a necessary part of the job - at least in the beginning - thereby choosing the path of least resistance, and in so doing finding one's freedom and rest in letting go to the ecstasy of breast-feeding.

One reason which is often cited for giving up breast-feeding is that women feel they have not got enough milk. It is an excuse of which relatives are particularly fond of. It is an obvious way in which to explain crying babies. They are hungry. Because new mum appears to be feeding night and day, and is unrested, she can readily begin to doubt her own body's capacity to feed her infant. This fragmentation of purpose and mental expenditure of energy in doubt and anxiety is what may cause the baby to be fretful and cry. It may even stop the baby from gaining weight and feeding properly. If the mother thinks she cannot nurture her baby, then the baby may feel this too. Breast-feeding is a totally telepathic relationship between mother and baby.

It is impossible to think that the baby is not synergistically connected to its mother. The baby depends upon its mother for its emotional learning. If she does one thing and feels another the baby will know. Often babies act out our own unexpressed pain. Your baby is your mirror. If she or he appears unhappy check your own emotionality. Are you in harmony with yourself?

Many Health Professionals in this country might argue that there is much work being done, in this country at least, to promote and encourage breast-feeding in new mothers. The British government have published a white paper in which they say they hope to increase the number of breast-feeding new mothers to 75% eventually. Whilst such a prospect is positive, the emphasis on the benefits of breast-feeding appeal to women on the basis of guilt rather than intelligence. A mother who does not breast-feed is made to feel inadequate and guilty that she is not doing the best for her child. But not only does the bottle-fed infant miss its birthright, which may create issues around his or her nourishment and ability to nurture itself later on, also the mother deprives herself of the deeply ecstatic nature of the emotional connection between herself and her baby as the milk (and love) flow from her breast through his/her mouth. Breast-feeding can be a deeply sensual experience if it is done with a spirit of total surrender to the flow of infant/mother harmony. There is nothing like it! Of course it is simply not always possible to go deep into this experience. There are many times when a mother just wants the baby off her breast and asleep so she can get on with something. Or just get some sleep. These are the times when she may think - if only I could give him a bottle. But it is still not worth trading the joy and healing of both mother and child, and the empowerment of woman that comes from her ability to nurture. These are missed moments. The baby will fuse with its bottle. Of course it will love its mother, but it will come to see a piece of plastic as the thing which can best soothe its needs, instead of the warm body it was once so deeply connected to. The warm body will in turn grow colder as it can no longer find the time to share its dreams and deep relaxations with the angel it has been sent for this purpose.

Besides this, bottle-fed babies do tend to follow a different sort of life than breast-fed babies. They are much more likely to become bottle-cot-bottle-cot-sleep-bottle babies than breast-fed ones who are more wakeful. Despite the apparent ease of bottle feeding, having done both myself, I can say that there is nothing more simple or soothing in the middle of the night than rolling over and putting a nipple in a waking baby's mouth. It is simply not simple to heat up a bottle of formula to the right temperature while the baby screams.

Women reading this who have not breast-fed their babies may be feeling very angry at the ecstasy they have missed out on. If this is the case I urge you not to become attached to missed experience. Ecstasy is still possible here and now. Breast-feeding is merely one of life's myriad opportunities to tune into the flow of the divine current. But that power is always there, it doesn't ever disappear, as we will soon see in subsequent chapters.

I myself have had great difficulty in carrying out this natural function, and it has taken me three successive births to heal the emotional scars of my inability to nurture my babies. As far as I'm concerned there really is no choice between breast or bottle, because they are not principles of an equal weighting. They are not choices about qualities of milk, they are not even really choices about infant food. They are choices about way of life and emotional connection of a woman. They represent a woman's ability to give of herself, and her compassion under challenge, and the resultant fusion and heart-centredness that comes from such unselfishness. In other words breast-feeding her baby is for the mother an act of power.

The beauty of breast-feeding is that it need not only be for food. Whatever the difficulties in producing milk, a woman who wants to connect, love and hold her baby can still do so. Even an empty breast can heal a baby, and feel good to its mother. The breast is an erogenous area.

The problem can be that if a very young baby is given a bottle of milk, it may lose the will to suck its mother's breast, especially if her milk supply dwindles. Nevertheless I was still able to do this with my third child and both he and I gained lots of love and healing from it. I wasn't producing enough milk for him to gain weight, for many reasons, anxiety of past failure, fluid imbalance, dehydration, weakness. I persevered for six weeks, but then I gave him a bottle (recipe later) but still breast-fed him at every feed. It worked almost too well because he is still breast-feeding as he reaches three years old, and I must write this book around his feeds. But I have finally reached the stage where I feel I have healed that damage in myself of not being able to nurture my baby, and I can look at another mother breast-feeding her baby without wanting to cry and if he were to stop feeding now, which ironically he won't, I would be ready.

Why not milk?

Cows milk is mucous and acid forming. It creates build-ups of fat. It is difficult to digest and is acid forming in the stomach. The spleen cannot transform it properly and creates dampness and phlegm, which is stored in the lungs. Frequent colds are the body's way of trying to expel this substance, which has become sticky and congealed. Milk is really an appalling food for humans, causing constipation at both ends of the body. The huge amount of children's respiratory infections that we see in this country are directly related to the excessive intake of milk and dairy products.

No other animal's milk is a suitable food for the human baby, and no amount of laboratory refinement can make it so. Of course babies (of all species) can survive and grow on milks from other animals, and sometimes there appears to be no other choice. But from a health point of view, the disadvantages of milk outweigh the benefits. So little of what we consume is assimilated. Contrary to popular and medical opinion, dairy products are not the best source of calcium. Just because a food is shown to contain a certain proportion of minerals and vitamins, does not follow that we can utilise that constituent just by eating it. What also counts is the suitability of the food for human nutrition, the quality and edibility of the food and under what circumstances it was produced. The marketing of products only emphasises the scientific results in its attempt to persuade us that a food is good for us. But if we are incapable of using our intelligence and body's wisdom to decide, then we will have to be responsible for the outcome. For example the recent campaign to promote Kraft Dairylea cheese portions as full of calcium, and therefore good for children, was either ignorant or downright irresponsible. Such a food - if a blob of processed fat and salt can be called that - does far more harm than good to the digestion of a child. Yoghurt too is marketed as a health food, along with images of slender, sporty people. But Yoghurt is a cold, damp food that turns into acid and mucous, and constipates us, unless it is very full of live acidophilus bacteria. Again, the emphasis on the bacterial properties of yoghurt is misleading, as there are other foods, such as Miso - an enzymatic ferment of grains and soya beans - that also do the same thing but are warming and healing in the process.

It is because Britain (and the West in general) is so meat, potato and veg obsessed in our diet that we do not have a proper picture of how to obtain our nutrition from the correct sources. Plant sources of vitamins and minerals are easily the best. They are the most readily digestible, the most easily assimilable, and because there is relatively little waste with them, the best for the health and correct functioning of the bowel.

This is not a book about nutrition and diet, but I do want to say that almonds and sesame seeds and seaweeds and dark green leafy vegetables are but some of the plant foods that are high in easily absorbable calcium. This principle works right the way through the plant kingdom, so you do not have to eat animal liver to get iron - liver contains all the toxic accumulations of the dead animal - cod liver oil is not the best source of vitamins A & D, and although animals are a rich source of protein, the quality of the protein is not compatible with human digestion in anything but the most minimal quantity.

A complete re-education of people as regards nutrition is absolutely essential.

On the other hand if people just paid more attention to their own bodily messages - illness is one such message - and developed their own bodily wisdom, based on how they react to foods, there would be no need for such an undertaking.

At the moment there is an emphasis on the allergic nature of milk. Divisions are created between those who are allergic and those who are not. The great majority of us are exhorted to carry on consuming the products of this multi-million pound industry, whilst alternative products - soya and goat's milk - are recommended for people who are desccribed as lactose intolerant. But it is not that simple. Everyone to some extent or another is going to have difficulty digesting cows milk. It is just that in some people, the signs of disturbance are more dramatic, or more marked. Moreover, neither goat's nor Soya milk are any more suitable foods, despite their nutritional constituents on paper. They are both also damp and cold and acid and phlegm forming. No, what is needed is a complete move away from the idea of milk as being such a vital food. But there is a major reason why this does not happen. Because we are as yet, a nation of infant souls, who need milk as a foundation of our culture. Milk is an immature food, used to satisfy the needs of hungry infants. It is because so many people have been so under-nourished, both physically and spiritually, that milk plays such a big part in our intake of substances. This indeed is one of the psychological reasons why milk is not a good food for us. It is because it is an infant food, that it helps to maintain us in an immature state. We must grow up. When human beings begin to depend less upon milk, so will humanity evolve to the next level of maturity. By giving up, or decreasing our intake of milk so will we be preparing ourselves for this stage.

So far I have shown how milk fails both in its health building properties and its psychological characteristics as an infancy food. However there is one further convincing reason why we should not use cows milk as a staple food in our diets. This concerns the karmic nature of milk production.

The spiritual aspects of taking the rightful food from the mothers of babies of other species, when we really do not need to.

By buying our daily pinta, we are condemning millions of dairy cows and their babies to a life of misery. The totally unnatural way in which cows are inseminated and milked, and in which their calves are raised, is a blight on the compassion and conscience of humanity. Housewives and mothers who buy their milk from the friendly milkman should realise that they are condoning and supporting a most unfair and sad industry. It is one thing to take a little of another animal's milk, sharing it with her own young, for our treat, but it is quite another to condemn a whole species to endless suffering just to support something we are well ready to give up. It is now time to wean the human species!

The Relationship of the Immune system to diet.

We are made of what we intake - constitutionally, physically and emotionally. Our children are, at least in part, what their carers feed them. Nothing builds a strong immune system so well as a strong healthy plant, grown without the use of artificial fertilisers or pesticides. Nothing is so damaging to our children's immune systems as the processed, refined, chemically laden foods, that are the staples of the busy mother's shopping trolley. Frozen foods, convenience foods, sugary foods and salty foods, all take their toll on the body's resources by draining vitality in the energy needed to digest them and the poisons they create in the body that are not being eliminated. It is only realistic to expect that outbreaks and epidemics of illness are directly related to the quality of food we ingest, and the environment we inhabit. If we want to have healthy, balanced children, then we must take responsibility for what we put in their mouths, and not succumb to marketing ploys, our children's trickster manipulations, peer group pressure or our own food compulsions and cravings.

So many harassed mothers give in to an, anything for a quiet life option and give their children food as an emotional fix. This might seem like an easy option at the outset, but when you are freaking out with panic in the middle of the night because your child seems so desperately ill as his or her little body tries to eliminate toxic material through disease, you will wish you had said NO. Balance and wisdom in the eating habits of the family are a better thing to cultivate. Children really do enjoy healthy foods, providing these are the normal foods eaten and no big deal is made about it. But a mother who does not value herself will not nurture herself, and if she does not nurture herself then she cannot possibly nurture her children. People need to pay attention to the quality of nourishment they choose because it is often directly related to the way they feel about themselves.

Conversely the more wholesome a diet one eats, the more whole one becomes, as the system begins to purify and the energy lightens.

There are still many mothers around who are convinced by the evidence of eating a vital, wholefood based diet, but who are running into a crisis of faith as regards immunising their children. Women have a lot of fear around this issue on both counts. Fear about vaccinating primarily, and the side-effects, both known and unknown, and secondly, fear of the consequences of not vaccinating.

Let me try to throw some light on the subject, as I am constantly being asked by women who do not know which direction to take in the question of immunisation. They are doing lots of soul searching. On the one hand they are being advised by the medical and allied professions that it is the most advisable thing to do. On the other hand, they are faced with the prospect of submitting their "healthy" child to a process that may deplete their health in the short term, in order to supposedly protect it in the long term.

What this thinking actually is, is a case of what the eye doesn't see, the mind won't know. Just because children don't get ill, because they have been vaccinated against specific illnesses, does not necessarily follow that they are well. It is quite wrong to think that immunisation will protect our children's health. It will not. What it will do is to stop them getting certain, specific diseases, that's all. That is by no means the same thing. There is even evidence to suggest that children may still contract the illness anyway, but that vaccination programmes merely prevent doctors from diagnosing the disease as such, which is then assumed to be something different. What we need to do is to consider the"cost"of protecting them against such specific diseases, and more importantly, to address the alternative methods of protection. Finally, should illness prove to be an inevitable fact and consequence of 20th century life on Earth, which I personally believe it to be, what are the best ways of coping with it for a mother who is experiencing the awful worry, stress and helplessness of having sick children?

A sensitive mother's instinctive protectiveness leads her to be naturally wary of putting anything that is not obviously necessary into her child's body, never mind possibly even harmful. It is a horrible thing to have to do to take your "healthy" child to the doctor's surgery, to have him or her injected with a substance that quite often causes some degree of sickness or unfavourable health reaction. It is also awful to have to watch something horrible being done to your baby, that will make them cry. Doctors and nurses know this and this is why they try very hard to convince us of the need to vaccinate our babies. There is an awful pull and tug on the parental heart strings, that goes on here, with mothers coming off the worst. If they don't immunise their children they will have to be strong enough to withstand the pressure of the medical staff, relatives, other mothers, school contacts and I told you so's. If they do immunise without full acceptance, they will have to carry the burden of their own guilt and lack of faith. Neither is an easy option.

Fortunately, the solution to the problem of immunisation lies straight before our eyes. We can stop buying into the belief system that says illness can and should be eliminated. That disease is a terrible evil to be wiped out and prevented at all costs. Even if those costs have not yet been collected, in fact have not yet even been counted. There is evidence to suggest that the debilitating disease of M.E., more virulent and less curable than has ever yet been known, is linked to the implementation of widespread immunisation programmes after the war. We do not either know for sure that the huge increase in Aids has not in some way been accidentally, some would speculate deliberately, genetically engineered by scientists in laboratories messing about with deadly toxic materials that have weakened our immune systems and our Earth's immune system.

The philosophy behind immunisation is very suspect as it attempts to control and defy nature. Illness is a natural life process which is absolutely essential in the maintenance of human balance. We become sick because our fine balance has been toppled by a number of factors. Illness is nature's way of allowing us space and the right combination of elements - e. g. heat, cold - to restore ourselves. The truth is that if we do not become ill, we die instead. Therefore vaccination is actually anti-life in its rationale. If we do not permit ourselves to release morbid matter from our bodies, it will not be able to escape, and will therefore poison us, perhaps slowly, but we will eventually become very toxic indeed.

Vaccination involves the forced direct input into the bloodstream of attenuated viral or bacterial material. The purpose of this is to "trick" the immune system into acting as if the body had contracted the disease already and to make specific anti-bodies to it, so that later on, should the child come into contact with the disease, its immune system will recognise the disease and already have the specific anti-bodies, in other words be immune to it. Because of the design and dosage procedure of immunisations, the child does not actually contract the disease at vaccination, but nevertheless we have to ask whether we believe that injecting morbid material into a healthy and very immature system, which is just starting to "kick-in" to independent life, is a particularly wise or intelligent thing to do? Do we really collectively believe that disease is so awful, and more importantly are we so arrogant that we would try to wipe it out?

One need only look at the decreasing levels of health, especially the increase in auto-immune deficiency diseases, combined with the massive increase in pollution and levels of stress over the past forty years, to realise that vaccination is no longer acceptable if we are at all concerned for the health of our children and the survival of the planet. Immunisation programmes are part and parcel of the Earth poisoning, anti-life thinking, that in its panic and fear of death, is actually hastening it.

Let us make no mistake about what is actually being done to our children when we take them for a "harmless" little vaccination. Their tiny bodies are having doses of "foreign" invaders injected, causing shock and imbalance to the constitution, and to the psychic and etheric and spiritual bodies as well. Side effects are the body's visible reactions to the trauma and may include rashes, diarrhoea, enlarged lymph nodules, screaming, pallor, blueness, limpness and fits. Moreover, the long term effects of immunisations are unknown. They really are a "shot in the dark". Is there any reason to believe that the immediate side-effects are the only side-effects?

I personally consider it an unacceptable and unethical

102

policy to carry out widespread immunisation programmes at this vulnerable time in the Earth's balance. It is the wrong way of going about the problem of outbreaks and epidemics of disease. It is simpler, cheaper and safer for the health and environment of the planet to boost immunity by correct nutrition, reduction of chemical and particularly synthetic, substances, and protection of the quality of the air we breathe.

Immunisation programmes, as an attempt to protect health, are like shutting the stable door after the horse has bolted. Adding further toxins to a world already drowning in poisons - remember The Persian Gulf, the Exxon Valdez, the beautiful Shetland Isles, the daily growing list of spoiled places - is not going to bring health. The worrying levels of pesticide concentrations in agriculture, diseases like BSE, Salmonella, Aids and so forth are all man made imbalances. Vaccinating against disease will simply drive the balance even further into decay and disease in the long run. By avoiding specific diseases we will simply give space to other more virulent diseases, in Earth's quest to let the steam escape from her boiling pot. Both ourselves and the Earth will need to become ill now if we are going to eventually get well. This is one of the laws of nature that no doctor or scientist can, try as they will, defy. It is a case of having to go through a planetary healing crisis, which I believe we are on the verge of, at this time in history.

Mothers and parents everywhere who accept the vaccination of their children need to think about what is taken for granted in that blind acceptance of science over nature.

In the first place we are saying, "I cannot cope with or accept the idea of illness. I believe it can be eradicated and my child need never be ill".

Secondly we are saying, "They know best. I am too frightened to face that my child may become ill. If I do not vaccinate my child I will not be able to go the doctor when he or she gets ill because they will say, I told you so, so I will have it done".

Happily, there is another option. Become one of the Medicine Mothers. Learn to be your child's healer. Become proficient in natural medicine yourself, so that you will never panic and lose control. You are your child's mother, the issue of your flesh. There need never be a separation imposed between you in health or in illness. You are both nurse and doctor to that child, and that is the way it should be. If you will no longer, as I suggest, buy into that system of fear, panic and poison, it therefore becomes your responsibility to understand the natural laws and to know in a simple manner what to do when your child is ill.

THE BOOK OF
THE HOLY FAMILY

Chapter 1
The Family.

The form and structure of the family must change

Children make a lighter impact on the world than adults. They are light beings, with tiny angelic voices. This is why we need to protect them from the heaviness and harshness of the energy of much of the outside world. Some adult energies are just so heavy they could kill a child. I have seen children frozen for a moment by a parent's rage. We can literally paralyse their energies, stunt their growth, if we are not careful how we handle our own energy around children. There is so much violence being done to children - murder, rape, incest, sexual abuse - but not all abuse is physical and most of it does not make the papers. As adults our responsibility is to raise our children without damaging them in body, mind or soul. As a practical task this is very difficult, especially where we are attempting to carry out this formidable task unsupported. Because the chances are that, despite our own efforts and control, most of us will sooner or later have to entrust a part of our child's life to outside agencies, such as babysitters, childminders, nurseries and eventually schools.

We need to learn how to be gentle with children. Our own children and all others. At the same time we have to teach them what is correct behaviour. Be gentle with your child. Remember, children have come straight from the source. They are in direct contact with the "home office" for at least the first three years of their lives. They can channel directly from spirit. Babbling babies may be mediums. Toddlers can access the genius of muses (remember Mozart). In touch with their inspiration, young children's creativity

108

can take them anywhere. How easy it is for frustrated parents to feel the pressure to "socialise" them.

From the earliest age our fear of our children's wildness and the social disapproval it creates, leads us to contain and placate them. We end up with children who are already out of touch with their truth by the time they are a year old. Food addicts, compulsive eaters, pudding babies, who sit saturated and zombified in their prams, their parents having traded their child's awareness of his own needs for a bit of peace and quiet. And then the neighbours will say "Oh what a good boy he is", except that behind your back they will whisper "oh what a fat baby".

Babies do not have their own aura (protective energy field that surrounds the physical body) until they are at least three years old. They must share their mother's aura. This is why it is so important to cuddle and hold and emotionally bond with your child, and anyone else's that you come across. Children are not getting enough love, and they cannot get too much! People who say you will spoil children by giving them too much love, are very damaged children inside themselves. You cannot spoil a child by giving too much love. The only way you can spoil a child, is by giving too much material substitution for love, as an excuse for not giving love. Too much food, too many toys, too many bottles of milk, too many foods for the emotional body. Love is the only food for the emotional body. Even the fattest of children can be spiritually and emotionally starving.

Normal children can be awkward and difficult, even at the best of times. The sheer pressure of bringing up children, and the attention that it is necessary to give them night and day, is too much for many parents. They are simply not able to cope with the needs of their children. We stand by and watch while these people get angry with their children. We watch them damage their children's spirits. We watch them try to extinguish their children's life sparks. Very often they succeed - the world is full of emotionally cut off children. I have seen so called 'naughty' children wither with shock under the force of an adult's unleashed rage.

Children give us a sense of responsibility that can, at times, be overwhelming to even the most dedicated parent. All you can do is to be your best, and know that your child has at some level chosen to incarnate to you, in order to undergo certain life lessons and experiences for the development of his or her soul. Therefore you are not to blame for your child's karma. On the other hand there are certain family traits and patterns that are both learned as well as inherited. It is the parent's task to be as loving as possible. In a two parent, nuclear family situation, a lot of responsibility falls to the parents, both to economically and emotionally prosper the children. The problem is that so many young adults are unable to do both, due to faulty upbringing themselves, that we have a situation of much anger, frustration and bitterness. The parent's dreams, if they had any, lie shattered in the effort just to survive and appear perfect, the happy shining family, in society's eyes. The pressure is just too much. I love my children dearly, but I do not think I could also thrive spiritually in a single family lifestyle. I want more than to be just the mother I would have to be, if I did not share my life with other adults. I need to do my own creative work, to keep my spirit alive. If I did not have the full loving support of other adults to share the upbringing of my children with, I would probably switch off, from the sheer exhaustion of my situation. It takes a saint to sacrifice her own path for the sake of her children. Fortunately, I am lucky enough to be able to link up with other adults, who share a common sense of purpose, to raise mine and their own children as whole and unscathed as possible in this largely very harsh world.

The separation and confinement of children into tight nuclear families, that is expected and required to maintain the patriarchy, is a prescription for the devaluation and diminishing of children. No one adult can be expected to give the love and attention that is necessary to nourish the open, innocent and expectant soul of a young child. I say one adult, because one if not both, usually has to be away at work in order to maintain the family's material needs. So the child does not benefit from getting the attention of both of its parents. So it all falls on one, usually, although by no means always, the mother. She needs to fill in her day with activities to break up the constant confinement with her child. Sometimes she snaps!

This is a heartcall to all mothers of cherubs. Our children will never be safe from harm until we live in communities of mutual support and can bond in love and sisterhood with other women. The nuclear family, with its intensity and confinement of relationship, is not conducive to the soul wholeness of the child. Patriarchy recognises this, which is why society has come up with the idea of school. School is not an enlightened answer to the stagnation of the nuclear family society that patriarchy gives rise to.

Nor is it a question of child-loving in this society, as to the reason why children are expected to be removed from confinement with their mothers. No. Patriarchy could not of itself, and by its own motives, care if a child lives or dies. But it needs future citizens to perpetuate it, workers and drudges to mindlessly rotate its laborious, tedious cogs. Patriarchy is male and militarily orientated. Its young must be made into its soldiers to protect it and fight for its perpetuation. Schools are the training camps of young patriarchal soldiers. Why else would children have to wear uniforms? If school is not a male device to get children away from their mothers, then why do little girls have to wear ties? School is the woman- hating solution to the problems and stresses of one parent confinement, that is considered important for ever decreasing age limits of children. It is almost a legal requirement of the system, many think it is, that mothers surrender

111

their children to be sent to institutions of socialisation, beyond the parent's control. The child's mind is then filled with the details that are thought to be important, and the values of the society of that day. In other words, woman-hating values. At school, the separation between mother and child is re-affirmed.

The woman-loving solution to the problem on the other hand, is the grouping together of women (and men if they are commited to their children) in creative communities of support. This is not just a question of women looking after each others children to give each other a break, although this is a start. It is about creating familial relations with other women. About trusting other women in friendship with your life and the life of your children. Our most urgent task at this time on Earth is to protect our children from harm. No one can argue that there is any safety for children from harm anywhere on this planet. Violence is being done to children from an everyday level, like a smack behind closed doors, to excision of the clitorises of whole nations of little girls, to ghastly and sickening murder of an individual or even whole tribes of children - infanticide. This is all going on all the time and we women sit back and accept it. Because we think we are powerless to prevent it happening. But we are not!

Violence to women and children is a fact of life under patriarchy. We think it sickening, but we have not yet changed the circumstances that permit it to be such a fact of life. Women and children are only able to be attacked because they are sectioned off, kept in mental and physical isolation within the family structure of patriarchy.

No one likes to complain. They cannot be sure that their experience is shared by other women because they are so removed from each other's true life experiences. So women are complacent to allow this to happen to their sisters and their nieces and nephews. Because no woman will get the support for interfering in what is considered to be anoth-

112

er man's business -i.e. his wife and children. We all suffer fear, but it is fear in isolation from other women. It is because we can be sure of being alone, behind closed doors, in empty streets, in deserted stations, hurrying home to our one and only lives, that we can be stalked and attacked. In the United States a rape is committed every 6 minutes. One out of four rapes have two or more assailants. What an easy target is a lone, separated, isolated woman, or child. Women can only be such victims of male violence precisely because they are isolated from other women. Cowardly men get women alone, away from their sisters and rape them. Other women offer protection for the single woman. A woman who is surrounded by the protection of her sisters cannot be victimised by brutality and violence. She need no longer be alone. In fact, if she wants, she need never, ever be alone again.

The protection of their children is not the only benefit of living in woman centred, child loving families of more than one woman. It is also about each woman being able to take what she needs from the relationship, within and because of the beauty of that relationship. Not only her survival, but also her personal and spiritual growth is addressed.

My 'sister, 'who is not my blood sister, but my chosen sister, or should I rather say my divinely sent sister, looks after and cares for my children as if they were her own. And they are. For while she is not their biological mother, she is their guardian and closest adult relationship, equal to me and their father. She feeds them, changes them, clothes them, educates them, gets up in the night with them, loves them and heals them. She is prepared to sacrifice her own time and self-centred creativity to them. And I mercifully get some time to heal myself and to write this book and their father gets some time to live the creative life he has been prepared for, rather than having to sacrifice his healing path to do a job he is totally unsuited for, and unhappy with, in which there is no growth, in order to bring home enough money for his children, his time with whom he has to sacrifice, during most days of their tiny lives.

This is the cruelty and the reality of the nuclear family situation that patriarchy virtually imposes upon us. It keeps the system going, but everybody has to pretend they are happy, because it is the only dream, the only relaxation and leisure patriarchy allows us - the nuclear family - and in it hardly anybody gets to do or even know their dreams. We are so busy just keeping up with the Jones', that we don't stand a hope in hell of really knowing who we are. We are mothers and fathers, wives and husbands, neighbours, workers, business-people and so on, but by the time the day is done, there is no space left to become ourselves, and this is why we are unhappy, angry and bitter. We must group together in new family bonds with other adults, whom we trust with our children, and within that grouping we may be able to find and express our individuality.

To devote yourself to bringing up your, or anyone else's, children unharmed, is truly Karma Yoga - the Yoga of selfless action. It is one thing to sit undisturbed beneath a shady tree and attain enlightenment, but quite another to gain your freedom whilst, and by, raising kids. Even the Buddha couldn't crack this one. He had to leave his family to find his freedom. The chances are, that by the time they have grown up enough to allow you any mental space whatsoever, you will feel too old and clapped out to start and live your dreams.

I believe that the secret of surviving family life, and gaining growth and liberation within it, is to have a strong spiritual life, and to use the time well to develop and heal our damaged Earth element, by doing simple things such as gardening, growing food, chopping logs, recognising the importance of life around the Hearth, to provide a beautiful creative environment at home. Whatever the family size, life should be lived as if it were a spiritual community, with the parents rising to pray and to chant and to do some exercise to keep fit. Then there will be more vitality to endure as the parents garner and harness the will to make their dreams come to life. Priorities and limitations need to be set with things like television and cooking, and above all, the parents must make time and space to be together without the children sometimes, in order to be grown up together and to discuss and harmonise their life-plans, or just to go out and let go together.

We need to still be able to have dreams and have children too. This is why we need other men and women who consider us and our children worth giving their love and devotion to. Those whose priorities are not necessarily to seek the perfect marriage and the perfect 2.2 family, although there's no reason why they can't have the cottage with the roses around the door. In return for their devotion, we share our lives with them;- our children, homes, ideas, love and money. We remain no longer cosy, isolated twosomes, engaged in war against all the rest of humanity, or perhaps each other. We become truly cosy tribes of adults and children sharing a balanced life with our children. A holy family.

At any time, any one of us has at least two other people to talk to. Two friends. Everyone is encouraged to their fullest potential, rather than the competition that happens between husbands and wives, and most importantly, the children are protected from the vibrational onslaught of the mother/father (male/female) split, that is the main defining characteristic of patriarchal society. What could be more healing from the mother/father abandonment than the lots of mothers/fathers family?

On top of that life is much more fun. Each day is different, there are always good things to look forward to, there is lots of happiness and no-one gets neglected.

THE BOOK OF
THE CHERUB

Chapter 1
Honour thy Children.

Pre-School, Post-parent children. Who wants them?

"Aren't they at school yet?" There is an implicit assumption that all children will go to be educated at school at an early age, and an almost universal acceptance that children must go to school by the time they are five.

Why must young children go to school, and why is there so much psychic sanction against those parents who are not convinced of the urgency of education outside the home.

The answer is quite clear. Patriarchal society needs to ensure children are "socialised". So priority is put on training the mind of a young child to emphasise the things that are important, such as being literate, articulate and able to compete in the world. The child goes to a place where it can be separated from its mother, home and siblings and where the priorities of the world outside are emphasised. Such characteristics as wildness and mischievousness are discouraged, as children are forced to compete against each other to gain brownie points of admiration from teachers and parents.

Natural spontaneity too becomes interrupted as a timetable of educational routine is imposed. I know there are many proponents of more child-centred education, such as Montessori or Steiner, but nevertheless these are still methods of teaching, which derive from certain beliefs about the nature of children and certain fixed principles of education.

Today's nursery schools are full of sad little children, who have been rejected by their parents. There are many hurt and saddened little children who are not getting the warmth and attention they need for normal, healthy growth. These are the children whose parents are not there for them emotionally or mentally. They are under-loved and under-stimulated and so they are sent to nursery schools in the hope that someone there will be able to provide the surrogate love, that the parents cannot give, because they themselves have not been loved enough as children. There is no healing at home because the parents have been so damaged by their own parents and so on.

So consequently nurseries become the day homes for many sad and depressed little children, for whom life seems to hold scarcely any joy. Is sending a small child of two or three away to school, five days a week, the best option society can offer at this time? Is it in the best interests of the child? The point is, in how many cases is this the best option and how often is it just that the parents are fed-up and want to shift the responsibility not only of looking after, but also of loving their offspring as well?

Obviously, there is nothing wrong with requiring space from your child in order to think and plan your own life. For many parents it is crucial. Children are very demanding. Neither is there anything wrong with sending your child to another safe place where it will gain social skills and stimulation. If you are committed to full-time work when you have young children then you will have no option but to find some form of alternative childcare. But nothing, absolutely nothing, can replace or compensate for love that the child is not receiving at home.

Young children know nothing about nurturing themselves. They are like baby lambs in a field, who need the security of their mothers and the flock, from which to be able to venture out. Of course it is good for children to have some social contact, to play with other youngsters, but it is quite wrong for them to spend so many hours of each week out of the nest. I believe the family is the proper place for young children to learn how to be human beings, not school. The parents, or those who are acting the parental role, are the ones who should teach basic values to these little more than walking babies, not some other paid person.

The fact is that most parents abstain from the task of educating their own children, often from the youngest of ages, because it is an awesome task and terribly time consuming. Most mothers cannot wait to get their infants off their hands and just get some space away from them, even if that time is spent at work. I cannot blame them for this, because it is also their need. But the sheer pressure and panic of trying to force little kids into the fixed rhythm of school is also a great responsibility and an obstacle to parental freedom.

Little kids flow, this is what their mother ideally teaches them, how to go with the flow of nature. One minute they are here, the next they are there. But the patriarchal school system is not about the little child's rhythm of flow and chaos. It is about routine and order, cutting off the flow of life and making things fit to rigid, linear patterns. Term time, school time, holidays, beginnings, endings, lunch, lessons, toilet. They cannot cope with it. Not until they are about 6 or 7 years old can children adapt themselves to a fixed rhythm. The system is designed to turn our beautiful wild angels into patriarchal soldiers, standing to the attention of an outside authority, being invisible, not a person, just a duty centred uniform, without its own face, without its own character and creativity.

Since all the weekdays are spent mostly inside a building, away from one's mum and familiars, there is no opportunity to do different or unusual things, such as accompanying mother or other adults on special occasions, or celebrating other facets of life that are not considered to come within school bounds. Flexi-school is almost unheard of, and commands much opposition when it is suggested as a possibility.

Part of the time at least children need to enjoy different experiences. But the idea of children not going to school at least some days a week is not developed. It's all or nothing.

How a child fares in this demanding situation is likely to depend more upon the gentility and decency of the teacher as a human being. Many teachers were bullied children themselves who were not respected. Some teachers have not yet learned how to respect children.

Schools that exist for the sake of the children are few and far between. They need our support and input as parents,if they are to fulfil their worthy mission to educate children,without harming them in the process. The sad fact is that the majority of schools exist for damaged adults, who are worried that children's nature may be too uncontainable, too expressed, too wild to be safe. So schools are designed like daily prisons for children to be incarcerated in. The environment of most schools is uncreative and unexpressive and even those schools that flourish like tough old weeds in a waste ground have a hard time maintaining themselves. Many schools have such appalling energy that children are actually being badly drained by the classroom environment. What is needed is a whole new child-centred perspective on the purpose and nature of education.

A sounder system of child care for youngsters would be a childcare-share scheme, operated by a group of mothers and fathers, whose interests would be primarily those of the children's well-being, rather than the economic motives that even the best-meaning nursery possesses. Mothers and fathers, rather than teachers, would be responsible for the care and education of young toddlers, on a part-time basis. So each child could be assured of full-time care, whilst each parent puts in part-time work, or income, depending upon their needs. These decisions would be able to be worked out by each group of people. The point is however that the children participating would have a sense of family from this type of childcare, which would operate from different homes, or a centre, and would experience the energies of different adults. This provides a calming, nurturing influence in which the child experiences family values, unlike the school based system, where the child is taught to separate from the family at too early an age.

Really what nursery schools often are, at their best, are therapy centres for children. It would be nice to see that the kind of places we send our children to during their "pre-school" years are those where the children's vitality will be increased rather than drained, and where the staff are themselves whole enough to be truly kind and to ensure the children's well-being, during the time they are entrusted with the little ones.

Education should be the food for the spirit .

I am concerned about the lack of spirituality in children's education today. Even those schools which attempt to be progressive have dropped the Christian bias in favour of the more politically sound agnosticism. But this does not represent a forward move, because while Christianity on the syllabus can represent a dogmatic insistence on the values and mores of the church, having no religious teachings at all fails to give children a rightful picture of their place in the scheme of creation. Moreover therapeutic spiritual practice at school, such as chanting or meditating, would increase the vitality and energy of our children, ensuring that they do not arrive home drained and depleted, as is the norm in the schools of today.

One of the arguments often put against including spiritual teachings in school, is that the family can provide the spiritual side of life. A school it is reasoned cannot provide everything, and parents have to do the rest. But the point is that children need to be shown that God is everywhere. Our spiritual needs are so great and so important that they must take priority above all else, and there must be no separation between home and school in terms of their divinity. The divine never stops and it is always there by our sides. It is us who forget the key to enter that door. This is why we must always remember to work at being in touch with God, and we cannot simply confine this exercise to several hours of the day. God must come first. Reading and writing second. Because without God by their sides, our children will not have a correct view of who they are and what is their place in the world. If the parents are the ones who show these values, they will not want the children to go daily into a space where these priorities are not shared, otherwise their children may start to undermine them and their way of life because of the lack of re-inforcement of these values as important. At this time, it seems the best option that one can hope for within the patriarchal education system, is one of the few kind, safe, schools with gentle principles and heart-centred values. However anyone wanting to live a full, vibrant, joyous and liberated life, outside of even the best of the constraints of societal norms and values is going to need the full love and support of other human beings, engaged in similar struggles.

Many communities of people living together have previously been conceived, formed and lived out. Some have failed, where their intention has not been strong enough to hold them together. Some are still thriving. A strong purpose to unite the wills of its members is an essential prerequisite of a viable community, if it is going to sustain itself and be ever moving towards freedom for its people. I can think of no more urgent purpose to unite us, parents and non-parents alike, than the protection and love of the children. They are our most important treasure. Their innocence and trust is unparalleled and we must do everything in our power to protect them.

Most spiritual communities, or ashrams, put the worship of God above all else. So do monks and nuns in their monasteries. God is sometimes too huge a concept for people to imagine, so often God is given a focus as his and her energies channel through a human link, an Avatar or Guru, who is often the most immediate and accessible figure of worship. Usually this supreme figure is the leader, or teacher of the community, in whose name the members may unite. This leader is considered to be closer to God than the others in the sense that he or she is the most spiritually liberated (enlightened) person around. Where children are brought up in communities of this sort, their quality of life, kinship ties with other children with whom they are not blood-linked, and spiritual teaching are unparalleled. However, the worship of God is still the focus. If God is seen as a power outside of oneself, the split between the God out there and the God inside oneself is reinforced.

What must now be established are communities where the intention of the shared lifestyle is the safety and happiness of the children. Communities where the children come first, in the sense that the adults group around them, in other words genetic communities, or new families. These can be as small as an extended family unit, like the one I live in, which can grow as new children slot in and new adults see the joy and freedom that they can find in the lightening of their load as they choose not to struggle on alone any longer.

God, far from being an inaccessible concept, is in the faces of happy children as they find their balance, within the safety of adult reassurance and support. By forming new families with others to nurture and foster the spirit of our children, whether or not we are the birth parents of those children, we are creating the strongest possible spiritual communities. We are embracing God's will.

Jesus said, " suffer little children, and forbid them not to come unto me; for of such is the kingdom of heaven." What he meant by this is that we must protect and love them, for they are holy and innocent already. They are close to God but also they are the creators of the future. If they grow up with a warped perspective, due to being damaged by we adults, there is no hope for the sanctity and well-being of this Earth, because they will not know how to care. Little children are about as close to the "Home Office" as you can get. We must honour the children, for they are sacred. Through the committed guardianship of them, we too will find God, as our frozen hearts and souls open up.

As adults working and living together we will be able to attend to child centred educational activities, whilst recognising that education is not just a question of going to school, but of using every life situation as a learning experience. Doing the shopping can be used as a valid maths lesson, as a walk in the countryside to pick herbs can be a lesson in biology. Because there are other adults to share the care of the children, no parent need miss out on their own work and activities, and there need be no separation between parents and teachers, because all adults are all. Whilst some should naturally be qualified teachers, others will simply be experienced in life, and can and should command equal respect.

Fixed principles need not be imposed because the nature of the education the children receive needs to take into account the flowing and ever fluctuating nature of life - the only thing that is constant is change. However there are some basic compassionate ideals that must be at the basis of any children's education. I would ideally like my children to go to a school that has been designed around our wholistic lifestyle, rather than our having to fit to the principles of the school.

Firstly, I choose to define education as learning about life, in its wholeness and all its glorious magnitude. It is as Miss Jean Brodie rightly puts it - "educare",(Latin) a leading out: not so much a putting in of knowledge, as a bringing out of what is already in there. Therefore, I maintain that any situation is valid for discussion and instruction. Life comes to meet us as it were. Therefore by sitting in a permanent classroom environment we are limiting our learning opportunities.

Secondly, I do not want or expect my children to be psychologically or physically harmed in the name of their education. Moreover, I actually expect their school to heal them.

Neither do I want to over-emphasise "gross" material values, as do most other schools. I feel they can learn how to be creative without lots of things. Results and classification of children into academic/non-academic (thick) categories is demoralising and life-purpose destroying. After all everyone develops differently and at different rates. Some people are tremendously creative, but unacademic, others are disadvantaged as children, but learn later in life what they are about.

I do not want or need my children to become institutionalised, and I do not want them to be made ashamed of themselves or their lifestyle as a common yardstick of normality is imposed according to the patterns of the majority.

They must be brought up with a correct diet for their health and balance, which is essentially a wholefood based, but not high in dairy foods, mainly vegetarian diet, according to the principle that food is medicine. They should not be made embarrassed or ashamed by their life-affirming choices not to partake of foods and substances that they know to be damaging.

All I ask for my children, and on their behalf, is that they have a creative space where they can play, learn and become "naturally" disciplined - that is according to the laws of what is good and right behaviour, i.e. non-harmful, non-aggressive and intelligent. They must develop their own powers according to their own particular attributes. If they are good at something, be it conventionally taught or not, it should be encouraged and fostered. Education is food for the child's spirit and the quality and variety of it is perhaps more important than the amount. What and how we teach it to our children is just as much part of their nourishment.

Chapter 2
Children and spirituality.

Are they compatible? Is it really possible to pursue enlightenment and have children? Can a mother become a realised being? Or are children and devotional life totally incompatible?

This is a tough question to answer. Because there can be nothing more frustrating than trying to meditate for example, when your children are around, which in the case of youngsters, they usually are.

Babies are a different matter. They sleep and feed a lot in the first instance, and during breast-feeding one can get into a deeply meditative and harmonious state with the baby sucking and sleeping peacefully at the breast. However, once they start to develop some individuality, it can be quite a different matter to get some peace in which to connect to one's own divinity. Children are exhausting and demanding and when they are young cannot really be left for a moment, for fear of getting themselves into danger.

If your meditation practice involves silent retreat from the external world, then there is no doubt that your attachment to practicing it will in itself be a cause of suffering, if you have young children. This is why it is so important to live in communities of support, so that there are other adults to watch the children while you go into silence. Alternatively you can grab your chances to meditate once the children are asleep. The problem may be however that by this time of day you are almost too tired to be bothered.

So many meditation practices involve renunciation of earthly functions and aspirations, including sex and children. So it is as if we have a conflict between practicing as a spiritual aspirant and having children. This perceived conflict can be the cause of so much suffering anyway, that the practice does not benefit one as it should. So one might as well not be so attached to having freedom and personal space.

In fact, it is by immersing oneself totally into the chaos and noise of children that one can find one's peace. This is the Zen approach to the question of children. Surrender your attachment to your private meditation space. Become totally involved in them, if you have no alternative, and in this fusion with your problem you will find the problem disappears.

There are many other ways of practicing spiritual life, without necessarily having to retreat from the world. With children it is possible to sing and to chant. In devotional singing one opens the heart chakra completely, connects with the divine source of all life and heals and entertains one's children.

The crucial lesson with young children is to not become attached to a method. Never let your vision of the divine slip, let the children be your teachers, there is no guru so exacting, so demanding and so honest as the clear mind of a child. Sing, chant and play and know that within these activities, and not outside of them, it is perfectly possible to find and love God.

THE BOOK OF
THE ORIGINAL WOMAN

Chapter 1
The Original Woman.

The original woman refers to a woman who is free of patriarchal programming. She acts from a place of truth inside herself. She does not, as does the patriarchal woman, have to perceive experience through a filter, which limits and determines her reaction and response. Original women are unbridled, uninhibited, unfettered, by convention or mores. They are not immoral, they are amoral. They are passionate women. They feel their feelings with great intensity, they experience their emotions and are truly able to be moved. They connect directly to their experience. Passionate, original women experience life directly and have the power to act as they see fit. They live from day to day, reacting appropriately, but not confinedly. They do not really care if anyone likes them or not, because they are the truth, and they reflect the truth. Many people are frightened of original women, because original women are weird. Original women are nothing if not original!

Original means first and earliest. It also means fresh and genuine. Another meaning of the word is the ability to think of, or carry out new and different concepts. Original woman is both the first woman and the new woman, because she is genuine and novel, the prototype of all women, as yet unconditioned to any expectation. She is woman before the system has been installed in the memory, pure and fresh. But she is also the woman who has stepped free from the chains of thousands of years of negative patriarchal mind conditioning and soul imprisonment.

Original women are original thinkers, whose feelings and passions differ from patriarchal women's passions, because they are always life affirming passions. Patriarchal women's passions destroy. Patriarchal women's emotions freeze up their energy, so they face the world as solid and still as if they were made from stone. If their passions cause them to act it will always be backwards actions, like revenge or reprisal. Their strongest feelings will be the patriarchally defined ones of hatred. The motive force for such wantonly destructive activity is a terrible lack of self-worth.

Patriarchally programmed women need to seek proof of their existence in the world outside, and can only do so by drawing attention to themselves for their most dramatic and negative acts. The punishment that is accorded, be it self inflicted or imposed by the judgemental society, gives them some feeling of existence, without which they are grey, unseen, invisible. It does not occur to them that they are able to interrupt the sequence and choose for acts of great joy and ecstasy, because their depleted selves have no knowledge of such great fortune.

The original woman can on the other hand walk head-long into her worst fears with her head held high, for she is never afraid to face the consequences of her life. She knows that by going to meet what causes her the most pain, rather than avoiding or denying it, she will, within that acceptance, eventually find wisdom, growth and liberation from suffering.

Many women are terrified of their originality because they fear no man will like them if they show any personhood. So they remain safely hidden within stereotypes and object to women who opt-out, who they reason must be lesbians, because they do not care about men's approval. So men and women alike reject the original woman, who has to withstand many crises of confidence and tests of her faith and determination on her road to freedom.

To become an original woman, if she was not always

one, she has to step out of the shadows of hatred, that is the mark of a woman who does not benefit from the perks of patriarchy, but is not yet either original, and turn off the manipulating negative thoughts of the patriarchally defined woman. She has to realise that she has power through her choice to live in self-definition, and that power is the power to love. When she realises that she has chosen to live her life in a way that allows her to be intelligent, so she can express that intelligence by not being drawn in to the clingy, infant-like behaviour of those women who need patriarchal approval for their existence. She can then meanwhile get on with her true God-given work and heal herself, the world, and those unfortunate souls who need her despite their inability to realise it.

Feminism is daring to become original

We have all been born into a world that defines men as powerful and women as not powerful. We learn that in order to possess power we must emulate men. Right now there are many opportunities about for us to emulate men and hence achieve more power than other women, at the huge cost of our originality. In fact this model of being a woman is what is popularly called feminism.

Of course this is not feminism at all, because the gain in this system is patriarchal power. Patriarchal power is "power over", and it is the unit currency of patriarchy. It is the carrot which has been dangling before us for five thousand years. At last women are getting a bite, and they are falling for the dodge. Patriarchal success is always measured in terms of competition. One always has to beat somebody else. But there is no power in damaging another's soul. There is nothing to be gained in squashing somebody else's spirit. Moreover you will be following that carrot for ever. If you are not tough enough to play the game you will lose, yet if you win, you will be ever scared of losing your gains, because nothing is based on your true ability.

As a woman competing in this system, your power over others is likely to be awarded on the basis of physical or external prowess. Either you look better than others, or you can do something better than others. How you are inside is likely to be a matter of very little consequence in patriarchal hierarchy. In fact quite the reverse seems to be true. Generally the more caring a person you are, the less success will you have and the least money are you going to earn. High achieving women in patriarchy tend to fit a model of womanhood that is far from original.

Women who graduate from the "Jackie Collins school of feminism" have mastered a model of womanhood that is seeking power over others, particularly men, at all costs. They are the ball-breakers. This is a particularly unfeminist model, because in order to exist it has to give consensus to the male view of power. It is a way of being that says men are powerful and so are we going to be, by using the same methods, only we can play dirtier.

This sort of perverse logic is very confusing to women and men alike. At this time, so many victories are portrayed as feminist, that are indeed only patriarchal reversals. True feminism is not about doing the same things as men. It is not about achieving equality in an unequal world. This just makes us as guilty as men in their uncaring, life destroying activities. No! True feminism does not buy into the same system as men, it does not accord with the idea of having power over anyone or anything else. There is power, but it is power from within the depths of one's being, power that originates from one's creativeness in the world. It is God-given power, in the sense that one gains it from one's own depth of connection with the divine source of joy and it is there to be shared, to bless one's fellow/sister human beings.

This sort of feminist power is energy. It is the energy of being in the world. Of being who one wants to be, and becoming who one has to become. It is the radiance and energy that emanates from a natural woman, who is being what she can be best of all - herself. Feminism is no more and no less than a woman becoming herself.

True feminism is by definition radical. Nothing other than radical feminism is feminism. All other sorts of feminism and things that are called feminist are patriarchal, because they buy into the male system by trying to find their place there, by attempting to force men to recognise women within male terms.

Radical feminism is not an opinion or even a view of the world. It is the truth! People are in such pain because the male/female balance is incorrect. We are like a ship going down that is over-weighted on one side. The only thing that can stop it sinking is to weight it quickly on the other side.

The Cult of the Cover-up girls

If the front covers of glossy women's magazines are representative of images of women that are considered attractive, fashionable and aspirable to, then we would all of us have to become ashamed of our intelligence. Just a glance at the faces staring out of the newstands of W H Smith, John Menzies and the like, show us that the women who are idealised as beautiful are empty women. The current model of an ideal woman is one who is childlike, haunted-looking and very, very empty - of emotion, of wisdom and of compassion.

The image of woman that is being photographed and distributed in massive quantities in every high street, is a woman with no depth of character, almost no individuality at all, whose clear eyes bounce right back into yours as you try to make some emotional connection with her.

We are idolising the empty goddess. The one who is cut-off from her feelings. She is unable to express her loving-ness, yet deeply needy of someone (preferably male, tall, dark and handsome and equally new modelish) to fill her gaps. She gives nothing, she only takes, because she is trained to be spoilt and selfish. So she pouts her discontent. She has self importance and believes she is God's gift to humanity. Yet her soul is not developed. If you don't believe me, look closely at the face of the cover girl. She is complete-ly outer, if you look deep into her you can see there is nobody home.

This can be very frustrating for the rest of us real peo-ple. Cracked and craggy women who nevertheless exude life energy and love. Because we are not given validity as beauti-ful representations of womanhood. We find it hard to find people who want our wisdom and our compassion, despite the fact that the world obviously needs it. Yet we are shunned because we name the pain of our lives, whilst ideal women cover theirs up, even to themselves. They belong to the association of those who think it a crime to acknowledge that their lives are painful. Thus their smiles, if they smile at all, are hollow and lightly mask over their anxious and buried internal pain. Yet they continue to play along with this game of unacknowledgement, until they become old and wrinkled and insecure, because they no longer feel they can exist without the shallow qualities time has robbed them of. Meanwhile the rest of us are derided and laughed at. We are called serious, ugly, manly, (worst insult of all), no fun, heavy, party poopers, wimps, blue stockings. Just because we acknowledge that life is a serious business, because we believe in people taking responsibility for their actions. Yes, we are deadly serious about life. But when we laugh, we truly roar with uninhibited laughter. Because it is laughter that comes from having suffered and having transformed our pain into art, into creativity, into love and compassion for others.

Ecstatica

It is time for us to honour the new front cover woman, to promote new models of womanhood to aspire to. Pictures of women who are bold and truly happy, but whose faces cannot disguise their lives. Faces of wisdom, faces of love, faces of depth and fullness. Faces that tell the true stories of women's lives.

Feminism is Re-writing history.

History is not an isolated subject that exists within a vacuum. It is not, as historians believe, an objective catalogue of facts. History is a record of the events and achievements of those people and events deemed worthy of remembering. We must realise that everything we call history is the history of men. Even the great recorded achievements of women have been achievements for the patriarchy - women saints, heroines, notable victims - none of whom have lived on to experience great joy and ecstasy.

They are all stories of women who have supported the patriarchal structure actively or by their negativity. Let us think of some of the great names of women in history:- Florence Nightingale, Boadicea, Joan of Arc, Marie Curie, to name but a few. What were their achievements? Weren't they all women in some form of renunciation - sex, children, life even? Apart from Lady Godiva, a sort of ancient Madonna type figure who rode naked on a horse through the streets of Coventry to shock people, aren't famous women in history all giver-uppers and giver-inners? Or male reversal female conquerors?

Historians of course have a bias. Historians are appointed by the livers of life to record their actions. Patriarchy appoints patriarchal historians to record the great events and activities of those deemed worthy and important. History does not record the history of birth and love and sex.

There are not millions of books on the subject. We do not study the lives of Original women for 'A' level.

No, history as we know it is the recorded activity of the male, of his great achievements. It is the history of battles and bloodshed, the history of destruction and death. It is the equivalent of the six-o-clock news from all times past. The history of suffering.

Women's history is the history of suffering, but also the history of love. The history of silent acts of nurture and care. All of which have gone on and on through history, in the background of those wars and conquests.

If we are to heal the despair and sickness of the world we need to realise that it is time to ask not only what women have been doing all these years, but also why isn't it considered interesting to most people? Why are our lives so unworthy, and so invalid to be recorded?

Even women have fallen for the sop, because we are not demanding to study our own history. Many women consider themselves uninteresting because they are having children and making love and raising families. They do not recognise their own history. But their history is the balance of the destruction/greatness principle which dominates this world. Theirs is the unspoken, unrecorded history of nurture and caring. We come across few true heroines in history because we do not support the view that a woman must either suffer or achieve in order to be great.

Humanity is in such an advanced state of social decay because the lives of women are not accorded respect by either men or women. There is no humility from men who are successful, even though deep down they are in discomfort because they "know" that they are not paying back for what they are taking. As each day goes on, the undercurrent of guilt increases, making bliss and freedom impossible to attain, as the catalogue of evil mounts. Yet ultimately there is only one thing that becomes worth having, and that is the ecstasy that comes from having relinquished all one's personal suffering.

Repetition of the name of the Patriarchal God fools us into thinking he really exists.

So many women are continuing in an attitude of silent suffering - only it is not really silent. It is certainly not peaceful. It is a protest that achieves nothing. It is power turned inward upon itself, power against, rather than power to change things. It feels negative, sucking and draining, and it attacks other women and even children, because it is indiscriminate in it's scope and it blames and attacks those who are not the target.

One can hear the anger in the tones and voices of women as they name the male programmes that they have been brought up to follow as accepted. It's St Patrick's Day, they might say for example. What about St Patricia? What the hell was she doing on that day? Well probably washing up after Paddy, so he could go out and be earmarked for ever as an important icon. We are all brought up to accept, to rote recite, to check other women, to train and track their minds, lest they forget that it is St Patrick's day or some other "important" historical demarcation. But there is anger in their voices, and maybe they cannot name it, that anger, but it comes from not being encouraged to have any mind space left in which to create alternative views of the world, while other women, it appears, can. It is anger at those women who are freeing themselves, while they remain mentally imprisoned. But it is misplaced anger, because it is not other women's fault that they are bound, and yet they are blaming them, and ensuring that they too must suffer. But this hatred just prevents them from discovering their own originality, until eventually the fear and resistance of creating any space becomes so great, because we are not sure that we will like ourselves when we see what has been buried in the pits of our unconscious, as it begins to surface when we start to contemplate. Because not only will we have to face the surfacing of our buried unconscious pain,but now we will also have to admit our hatred for other women. This will be even harder to accept if we have called ourselves feminists. But a woman who does not love herself, cannot possibly honour her sisters.

Another example of our assumed dependence upon the male model of life relates to our health. Everywhere you go, women are always talking about going to the doctor's. It's like our religion. Why do we women assume we need a doctor at all? Is the thought of taking responsibility for our own and our children's wellness so terribly daunting? Does it demand so very much energy of us that we would rather suffer the sometimes dreadful consequences of submitting ourselves to medical scrutiny, often at the slightest cause? It's as if we have this logic yardstick that we use to measure our health. If a doctor says we've got cancer, then we'll just curl up and die. We'll submit to painful and poisonous radiotherapy, and either be drained and ill as hell, or try to keep up a cheerful front, whilst inside we are paralysed by our fear. But if we feel ill, and it's not diagnosed by the "experts" as terminal or serious, then we'll try and pass it off as unimportant in our own minds because we know it won't kill us.

I am upset and frustrated at the way in which women willingly submit themselves into the hands of people who they consider to know more about them, than they do themselves. And in a certain way they do. Because women will not take that responsibility to learn. We hold the mistaken belief that there is no joy for us in learning about ourselves. There is a terrible fear of the shadows of one's own darkness. It is all considered to be too awful. So we will continue to suffer. But let me say this. The pain of ignorance and fear is much worse than the pain of illness. There is joy to be found in the acceptance of suffering illness, whilst knowing you are healing at the same time and that your belief in your wellness is your burning light. It is worth believing in your power to be well Even if you are dying. Even more so if you are dying. There is a sad, but ultimately glad truth that is inescapable in this world. Try as you might to run away from yourself you cannot. Therefore experience the joy in facing up to yourself - Warts and all!

Chapter 2.
Womanpower.

Who will be the new agents of post-patriarchal consciousness? Once we, women as well as men, are able to open in worshipful ecstasy to another woman's being as well as to a man's, then will the world become a safe place, and a happy and joyful one.

We are born into a way of operating that predetermines a reaction to another woman as either hostile or patronising. She may be the most powerful Goddess/Healer that you have ever come across, but you will be too blinded by your antagonism to see this. If you think she has succeeded where you have failed, you will hate her, at least unconsciously and you will think negative thoughts to try to 'bring her down to size'.

Many of us who think we are liberated can go to sit at the feet of a woman guru who asks nothing of us, than that we love God. Who is God? We have to give up nothing of ourselves in such a quest. Shaving our heads, giving up eating meat, smoking, being kind to old people. These sacrifices are not acts of power. What really counts is being brave enough to dump your pain. To give up whatever is required of you personally, where you are making your negative causes in this world. To be prepared to make a difference, in whatever way you are requested by the divine power to do, in order to usher in the new era. If needs be, you must dare to be radically different, because you dare not, not be. For it is only in the embracing of non-patriarchal, post-patriarchal reality/life, that we will be free to keep our sanity, in a totally insane world of despair, misery and depression. (The doubtful might just watch the news tonight!)

We probably will not choose to follow this dictate in the first instance, because we will fear to surrender what we are obliged to lose. But what we'll be going to lose is only our self-hatred, our sister hatred, our woman hatred and our man hatred and it is damn hard to name it, to uncover it and to eject it from our little woman computers. But when we do eventually complete that task, there is nothing waiting for us but happiness, and more importantly, freedom!

You may not be able, like I was not in the first instance, to choose for happiness. Perhaps you are in too much pain, too much rage, bristling with anger and blaming for your life. But the chance will come again and again, and then you will take it, because you will be ready to dump your struggle, and give up your ego. Especially if you are about to lose everything you truly care about, if you do not.

It doesn't matter if you cannot choose for happiness as long as you choose for power. But in the end you will find your happiness in that choice for power. By power, I mean your own personal freedom as lying in harmony with the freedom of the planet from all human imposed suffering and bondage.

The power is there for the taking. There is no one who can stop you from becoming your whole, magical self, - except of course yourself! Patriarchy is not people, although there are key characters in its perpetration. But there is no one Mr Patriarch, who sits at the top. They think there is, but I will tell you categorically, his seat is vacant. The male God seat is empty. It is illusion, a myth.

Therefore, providing you are a warrior in your life, a woman warrior, and do not fall in, in any way, with those people or energies who can harm you, the radiant channel to freedom is clear up ahead.

What is patriarchy?

What is patriarchy? Patriarchy is a "reality" structured by one condition of the external mind. It is the very essence of fear, fear to survive. It is a set of thoughts, beliefs and feelings (a set of commands) that stem from the need to compete to survive. It thrives on huge often unspoken fears that if we do not compete we will not have sustenance. It is an uncontrollable virus, that eats away at our system. It is a life response that separates and fragments, causing us to feel separate from each other, from the environment and, naturally, from God. Nevertheless, in spite of the pain of our lives, we still almost all give our continued consensus to this way of being in the world, which leaves us with a great, huge, yawning cavern of longing that must be filled.

It is the reason we feel so desperate to fill up our lives, with things, with sensations, with people and emotions or substitutes. Because we all feel unloved. This is because humanity has not yet learned how to love, not yet collectively opened the heart chakra, due to fear of the consequences and pain of doing so. So fear of love is at the root of patriarchy, that binds humanity, including and especially, women, children and animals to endless suffering. We have not yet learned that we are indeed not separate individuals, and that despite our resistance and insistence to the contrary, there is really no such thing as "I".

People who have experienced deep states of meditation or dreams come to realise that there is no separateness in the reality of existence, everything in life is interconnected, interwoven, spun by the web of Spiderwoman into one seething, pulsating, ever-moving and changing whole.

"In higher states of consciousness we would see that we are not just linked with the minds of the world, but also

the minds of the world of unembodied souls and all the levels above. It is not a thinking or feeling , but 'a being'. Like one blood cell in a giant vascular system". Goloka Om. (Jade)

But because we never stop ourselves for long enough to experience these more subtle energies, we don't realise this. We have not seen it with our own inner eyes. We live our lives from a total self-centred perspective. For us, there is nothing beyond "I" Yet the truth of the reality is that there actually is no "I". What we truly are is only accesssible beyond the "I", yet most of us will never get there. There is no time for love, because we fear that if we stop we will starve. We are all left with the ever present fear that we will be on the streets if we stop buying into the system of competition and greed. We have no idea even that it is possible just "to be", without wanting, needing or thinking anything. Just to be happy inside oneself, to be content and complete inside our own skin. Because if we if we drop out of the game of thought webs that we are intricately tangled up in, we fear we will be homeless, moneyless, deprived and poverty stricken. So we trudge exhausted ever onwards on the wheel of suffering that is the only outcome of mundane existence and the denial of a spiritual life that characterises patriarchy.

But we must stop. Stop the wheel. More and more, as our lives evolve, we need to delve deeper into the real world and leave behind the mundane world. Because what we have come to call reality is merely the limited set of thoughts and actions that we know as patriarchy. And what we fear and resist is the unknown space within us that is not patriarchy. Yet we claim to be feminists and resist all that is patriarchal. Therefore we must without fear attempt the great and inspiring work of undoing all the threads that bind us to the wheel of suffering.

Economic power: The need to use money in
original ways.

Women who have access to any economic power under
patriarchy must realise that there is an expectation that they
will use this power to perpetuate patriarchal status and hierarchies. All money is patriarchal money. The whole concept
of the need for an external measure of wealth is divisive of
people. We are deep in an economic system that is
entrenched, and whether a woman's money to live on comes
from a father, husband or the state is irrelevant. Even if she
earns her own wealth through the direct fruits of her own
labours, the money she has access to still comes from an
agreed, consensus model of economics which she has had to
participate in, in order to" bring home the bread". All this is
a source of conflict and separation between women. Better
off women are hated by poor women for having money, but
all money is a patriarchal concept, and since we need it to
purchase quality of life, we had better accept it at this time,
whilst preparing ourselves to live with increasing simplicity.
What is truly important is not how we make or get money,
but how we choose to spend and distribute our wealth, and
whether and with whom we choose to share it.

It is time for feminists to stop agonising over the ethics
of wealth and to realise that it is possible to have money and
to be a feminist because one's feminism shows, not in not
having any money, but in the way we use it.

We need to simplify our lives. For simplicity however,
do not necessarily read anti-technology. Simplicity means to
question our needs, and to use money wisely and to make
intelligent material choices. To live within our means and
according to our needs. But pleasure and leisure are needs,
as well as food for survival and a roof over one's head. It is
not necessary to reject money, to turn our backs on it in order

to prove we are feminists. We do need to use our money in feminist ways - that is to create a positive loving world, and to give chances to those who might not otherwise get them, within patriarchy's cruel status system. So original women need to lose their fear, to stand up and be counted, to express their choices freely in life partnerships and relationships, to lead the way in ushering in the new order.

It is not practicable to do without money at this time, if such a choice is a choice for a life of suffering. I believe there will come a time when money is no longer valid as a human currency. However that time is not yet here. It makes sense to prepare ourselves for survival without money in the future. Exchange of skills and resources, where possible and practicable, is a very positive thing to do and we need to practice for the future, so that we could survive if we had to, without funds. We need to be the leaders, at the forefront of a humanitarian movement to exchange with others. I think such systems of barter, which were once so common, will come again in a new form with new priorities. Money begins to lose value in life, as spiritual qualities take precedence. True life qualities and abilities will become recognised as the needs of tomorrow.

Acts of power: Original women do sacred work.

It is important to discover your sacred work and do it. Your sacred work is like your medicine. It is your mission. It is what you are here for. Sometimes women who know what they should be doing still cannot muster the courage and will to do their sacred work, because of their doubts and lack of faith in themselves and their work. It takes belief in oneself to do one's true work, because patriarchy conditions us as regards the work that we choose. If we use the patriarchal value system on which to base our lives, we will be discouraged from doing our sacred work. This is the point at which so many women get stuck, in the fear of not having our needs met, especially if we have children. But it cannot be right to remain frozen with fear as we give in to the tyrannical power of the patriarchy and surrender our life work, hopes and dreams. We simply have to believe that if we do what is our calling, we will be protected. We must overcome the fear and believe in our own power and will and strength to survive. Nothing is worth compromising our life energy for, nothing can be worth freezing up our lives for. Surely there must be a way?

I feel that producing this book is an aspect of my sacred work. I could and have fallen at the first hurdle a million times. My faith has been my stumbling block. But I plod on, because when you have discovered your sacred work, any other work is a waste of your life.

I believe that if we do our sacred tasks, with true faith, we will always be protected. We will find that the positivity of our purpose attracts us enough money to meet our needs, and we will be looked after materially as we amass the spiritual fortune that comes from committing ourselves to the healing that following our destiny brings. No matter what our sacred work is, there is nothing in the patriarchal work world to compare to it, and the benefits that doing it will give to you and humanity. But you will need to convince yourself that your work is valid, and to overcome your anxiety that you will not be able to survive if you do not struggle along in the patriarchy, and to start believing you will.

I feel it is really important for us to stop giving consensus to the view of things that says we can only survive by competing. By tapping into the powerful mystic law, and moreover putting our faith in its power, which is true power and not 'power over' - as is the currency of patriarchy - we will find friends who are able to help and support our endeavours. It may seem difficult at first - we may need time

to go wholeheartedly into sacred work. It may be appropriate to continue working within the patriarchal structure for a
while, just until you can build proper bridges to take you
safely to the sacred side of the river. But don't get caught
procrastinating for too long, or you may miss chances to do
your work, because of your fear of launching yourself.
Whatever you do, you must keep your purpose foremost in
your mind, and it will naturally grow, until the time when
you are free to do your sacred work wholeheartedly.

It might be appropriate for you to group together with
others in community. Help other women to do their sacred
work. This will bestow great benefits on you and help erase
your karma and heal your pain!

Don't be so attached to doing it all "on your own". It's
impossible under patriarchy for any of us to achieve enough
prominence with our sacred work, to give us the feedback we
deserve. Impossible for us to gain access to enough lines of
communication to spread the word of happiness to other
women and suffering beings.

So we must put aside our own needs and help others
who have a strong purpose - because in so doing we will
grow and heal.

What is our sacred work and how do we find it?

Sacred work is work that liberates the spirit and frees us
from suffering. When we do our sacred work, we heal as we
release our pain and anger. When we do our sacred work we
do our art. It is the work that inspires us and others, and
which makes us feel whole.

It may be a while before we discover our true purpose.
We need to be open to it for a start. We will know when we
have found it, because it is work that is not tiring. It does not
drain us. We will be able to look at the fruits of our own cre-

ativity and wonder - did we do that? Each day, our labours will grow, little by little, until they have taken firm root in our lives. Then when people ask us "what do you do?", you will be able to answer with confidence based on belief in yourself, "oh I'm a ...."

This work will not be your job, as is patriarchal work. It will be your work, which is quite different, because you will not dread it, although you might find it hard to get down to. But once you are immersed in it you will lose all concept of time and tea breaks. Sacred work is like meditation, you may resist it at times. Be aware that those are the times when you most need to go and immerse yourself in it. From this deep dive into the thing you most resist, comes knowledge and clarity.

You will find your work in your open heart, and you will open your heart through your sacred work. You will also open your heart through your meditation and the power of your spiritual practice. You may know what your sacred work is all along, but it may be that you will not find it until you have found the key to becoming whole. That key is the unlocking of the door to ecstasy, which is a high state of being but where you are totally clear, grounded and purposeful, based on the pleasure of the depth of your inner self. Ecstasy is not to be mistaken for euphoria which is ungrounded, uncentred highness due to an outside trigger - rapture. In releasing suffering you will fill with ecstasy, that is the glorious experience of being totally free, having dropped all the constraints that you have imposed upon yourself. In this level of being you will locate your sacred work.

But first you need to do your spiritual work on yourself, healing and facing up to who you are and what you have allowed to happen to you and what you have created for yourself. This is when you may need to be supported or may have to keep up your patriarchal work. This is the period of transition. It is easy to lose one's purpose and clarity and get waylaid or undermined at this stage. It is rather like giving birth. Transition can be the most painful stage. But it is important to keep up, because you are nearly there. Once you have reached the point of being able to accept yourself and yet love yourself, in spite of what may disappoint you about yourself, because you do not doubt the depth of your commitment to life, then this is the point of no return, at which you will start to diminish if you do not do your sacred healing work. Once you have found something of benefit to do, then you need to do it, and you will find that once you harness the will to start, everything will support you in that choice. Doing your sacred work may mean you doing your act of power, which may be by no means an easy thing. For even when you know what it is, it is quite another thing to muster the strength of will and purpose, the commitment and faith, to carry it out.

It is so easy at first to go off the track of power. To lose your way on the path of power in a host of mundane distractions. You have probably gone off the route many times, as if it were not the most important thing for you in the world right now. Enough people are angry enough with us to stop us psychically from achieving our acts of power, as it is. No one who is not living their dreams is going to want someone who is close to them achieving theirs. This psychic blocking makes it easier for you to get distracted. We don't want to attract jealousy or disapproval.

Even though you may not admit this is happening on one level, it will still serve to block you from carrying out your task. But then you need to learn to recognise the warning signs of having left your path, such as nameless depression and anger, sapping feelings of quiet despair, and to realise it is because you have allowed yourself to wander from your purpose or to doubt its validity, and you need to get back on your path as quickly as you can, because your path is your fastest way home to the unbroken, undifferentiated, ecstatic consciousness otherwise known as God.

One of the biggest blocks to becoming original is our FEAR. It's such a big one, because even when we think we have lost it, it still can rear its ugly head over and over again. It permeates our lives, in our thought processes and our lack of decision and action. What is this fear? This cold blanket of low life state emotion that sweeps over us like a mist descending on the moor? Where does it come from, this reaction that makes us say no when we mean yes. That makes us choose for limitation and immobility, instead of for growth? Is it a fear of meeting up with ourselves? Fear of facing our own shadows? What are our shadows and where do they come from?

I believe our shadows come from our need to control reality, where we fear we may be left behind if we do not. The only cure for this malady - for this is what fear is - is to let go, to surrender humbly, joyfully, totally to life and love and let the emotion of your surrender wash over you and engulf you in its power.

The need to control was put there by the patriarchs, because if you were to let go of your pain, you will surely find ecstasy in that surrender, and if you find ecstasy you will dump your struggle. You will no longer be a patriarchal soldier and spokesperson, because you will truly have discovered the smallness of patriarchal reality. Having discovered what size life can really be, you will no longer be content to suffer for the miserable pay-offs you have been receiving for your acquiescence. You will instead want to become spokesperson for the other side of life, because you will want to share the great news that there is joy in the universe and everyone can have it. There is loads of it, it never runs out and it is just the other side of the clouds of your consciousness. With determination and positivity we can disperse these clouds, but it is a matter of growing our faith strong enough to believe in the positive nature of this message. After lifetimes of suffering this may just take a little time. Or it may not. However once we realise that we do not need to suffer, and that it is moreover spiritually quite inappropriate to suffer and does not benefit us, others or the planet, all of whom are suffering enough already, then we can make the choice to let go of our despair, and re-programme ourselves for happiness.

THE BOOK OF CUPID

Chapter 1
Healing our Sexuality
The Second Coming.

When we connect in sexual fusion with our lovers, we open ourselves to fusion with the universe. By aligning our total beings with others, we open the pathways to the angels. We open the door to another level, a level of being that exists simultaneously but that we cannot always find the key to enter. The message to women is loud and simple - WE DO HOLD THE KEY.

By fusing and connecting the pathway of the chakras from the root to the crown, we become open and able to travel to other realms. From our bottoms to our tops we open and join our totality to that of another and hence that of the huge power that we are all a part of. We enter and experience the God realms, where all entities are one. We are no longer perceiving ourselves as separate beings.

This "space of alignment" is where all times are synchronised and linear time does not exist. One cannot tell where one ends and where eternity starts, because you are one and the same, totally wrapped up in a cushion of ecstasy. This is where Cupid waits in the wings, to grab lovers and heal them as they touch the realms of this space. It is also where the angels are waiting with the souls of babies who are to come in through this gateway, for it is also the entry point for new life.

When we fuse in tantric communion, holy communion, that is characterised by ecstasy, we are able to become totally embraced by cosmic consciousness. We are, as it were, in God's duvet.

Orgasms are one way to break through our blocks to release ourselves to reach this pinnacle. Multiple orgasms are one of the keys - that is orgasms to a point of optimum healing - where knowledge can be gained. Women need to realise, that while it is wonderful to come, once may not always be enough to experience the ultimate states of ecstasy - the point where there is knowledge of other realities. We may need to have multiple orgasms to open ourselves further and fully into ego-lessness.

The way to have more than one orgasm is to surrender totally to whatever waves of pleasure and emotion your body experiences. If you reach orgasm, open to it totally and embrace it. Once your orgasm is complete, relax and let go again. Do not attach to the first orgasm, no matter how ultimate you felt it to be. Have no thought about it, just relax and let it start to build up again. It will, because women are designed to have several orgasms, whereas men can just keep going until they climax. It will be possible to achieve more orgasms and become more totally fused, until you reach a point where you are in angel consciousness. But please do not be attached to having this experience, every love-making is different, and everybody's experience will probably differ. The main thing is that you surrender to the power of your love and emotion and that you connect yourself more and more in fusion as your blocks drop away through the rhythm of your pleasure build up.

The point is, that when lovers connect and relax into each other,with deep, unhurried breathing, there is nowhere to go. There is no frantic peak to be reached, because once one has reached the peak, there is only down to follow. In tantric sex,there is an acceptance and embracing that occurs, that doesn't happen in the frenzied sex experiences that we usually see in movies and on TV. Love making, means making love by having sex. But we so rarely see love being made. We have come to see love making as an act, making orgasm. Then when it is over, the couple light cigarettes, turn away, roll over, go to sleep. They have relieved themselves of their tension, if they are lucky they have made a little love. But that is what sex should truly be - making love. Creating love as a meditation. Building love, not necessarily excitement. Building and growing love to the brim. So that the lovers remain bathed in the radiant light of love and ecstasy. This sort of sex is not a needing, it is a healing. It makes the lovers whole. It is one of the most powerful, easily accessible means of healing that we have available today.

Many people on the planet today are healing issues of second chakra damage - sexual abuse, trust abuse, love abuse. Explosive sex may be, at least initially, important to heal this damage. Passion is the cure for frozen hearts.

Most tantric teachings that are practiced today have a patriarchal bias. Their notion of orgasm is that men and women need to hold off climax and build up to an ultimate peak. But I feel that if women hold onto their orgasm, they may in fact not be accessing and connecting to angel space, because the multiple orgasm is a trigger. As I said, we already hold the key to ecstasy.

Yet we poor women are living in such pain and unhappiness because we are not "turned on". In other words, our energetic frequencies are not aligned with those of the Earth's and as such we are not able to heal the earth. It doesn't matter how liberated or how feminist we think we are. If our anger prevents us from experiencing the sacred healing force of ecstasy, then we will not be truly happy. It is the force we are all seeking.

Women are very confused about our sexuality. Many of us have allowed ourselves to become "token torturers", harsh judges of other women's morality. We act as agents and perpetrators of patriarchal oppression, as we persecute other women who we consider to be too sexy, and hide our own sexiness. We deny our own desire for pleasure, our natural, healthy, divinely bestowed gift, in the hope that we will please society. Then we wonder why our male partners go off and have affairs! Others of us are making the mistake of looking to a partner to give us ecstasy. Most of us women are searching for the man who can turn us on, who can switch on the bliss for us. We are either denying our sexual selves, or looking for a man to press the on-switch. But ecstasy is not a thing that we can be given. It is a power that stems from within each of us, from deep within our chakra bodies, and it comes from our own love and delight at life, the opening of our hearts as we synergistically vibrate with creation.

There is no reason at all for any woman to be unhappy. All the pleasure circuits are nicely installed within our own bodies. We come complete with system software. (Perhaps the unacknowledged recognition of this inborn power lies at the basis of female genital mutilation practices in some parts of the world.) Thankfully, the majority of us are untamed. We are able to orgasm with or without a partner. We are able to be rude and lusty, wild and wanton with ourselves. What fortunate creatures we humans are.

Ecstatic sluttishness is not the same as depraved sluttishness.

We have such a negative imprint of sexuality as shameful, that we need to learn to distinguish between ecstatic sluttishness and depraved sluttishness. The former has self-respect as its basis. Ecstatic sluttishness refers to the lustiness that a woman feels about her body and her partner's and at the thoughts of the wonderfully exciting and rude things they can do to stimulate and arouse each other. Depraved sexuality however has lack of self-worth at its base and is patriarchal. Ecstatic sluttishness is for one's own and one's lover's pleasure and one's own joy, although not exclusively of course. It is a means to heal oneself. It is sex with the heart open, and it is receptive. The build up of joy and pleasure can lead one to fusion with the divine, through fusion with one's partner, by acts of love carried out in the spirit of humble surrender to the greatness of the force of divine love.

Depraved sluttishness on the other hand, is a way merely of punishing oneself even more than usual, by allowing oneself to be used for someone else's fulfilment. It is not characterised by ecstasy, although there may be pleasure, but there is not mutual love, therefore it is not a warm and healing pleasure, but a depleting pleasure. Here, a woman is just giving her vagina to the act, but not her heart, brain, soul, body, every bit of her being. Depraved sluttishness is making love with an attitude of need, or fear and self-denigration, competition or conquest. By surrendering and offering every bit of yourself to love, you are allowing yourself to open the doorway out of yourself. The key from depraved sluttishness to ecstatic sluttishness is in loving yourself and loving your lover/s. By giving to others at the expense of yourself however, your self-esteem drops and you feed your guilt. Instead of being refilled, you are left empty, like a used bag.

All that is the difference between the two sexualities, is your attitude, your feelings about yourself, where you are coming from, your sense of self. If you approach sex feeling worthless and a victim of your life and your partner, you will not benefit from the healing force of sex. Sex will weaken you and cause you suffering.

The difference is in the quality of connection. To experience tantric communion in sex means to be able to let go of all the insignificant things in one's head, and not attach energy to passing thoughts, but simply get on with loving our lovers. This means allowing oneself to fuse at all levels. In the genitals - feel the lustiness of that connection - in the heart, this is where ecstasy flows from and through, and in the brain, with total telepathic lovemaking. But never forgetting our worshipfulness. Sex allows us the chance to express our gratitude to the divine for our lives and for being so fortunate as to be able to experience such love, with our beautiful partners. In ecstatic sex we can express our highest being. Ecstatic sex is truly holy.

But as long as we expect our lovers to do all of it, to give us ecstasy by their ministrations and stroking of our egos, we are sunk. That love must spring up from within each of us, it is our divine spark that grows and grows as we appreciate and wallow in each other's holiness and spirituality. As we make love, we make love with God. We can see our partners as beautiful holy men and women, gods and goddesses, but we must also must come from a point where we are seeing ourselves as gods and goddesses too. Woman's sexual misery is to expect men to see them as goddesses when they do not themselves have this belief as base.

It is within our own power, in our own true and well-founded view of ourselves that our capacity for ecstatic sexuality lies.

Wrong identification of "the Lord" is woman's pitfall.

We tend to "fall in love" with a man and give our all to him in passionate love making. But it is him that we surrender to, as we allow ourselves to open in emotional fusion with him. We worship him as our God. But if he then leaves us, we are left hurt and completely bereft. This is because we have wrongly identified our lover as the source of the bliss and cannot see that the true source of love is in fusion with the divine. We have therefore become totally dependent upon our partners for the source of our divinity. So if they leave we allow them to take away our connection to God, or

163

so we feel. This is wrong identification of the spiritual source of life. We have confused lust and love.

We must realise that we can connect directly with the divine source. It can help us to have the channel of a human partner, who can act like a transducer for divine consciousness, but it isn't the only way. We can receive God's love directly and must make no man (or woman) the source of it. We can be in love even without a partner,and indeed this is the whole point of tantric fusion.

Until we discover our wild woman selves, until we become strong in our sexuality, by our power of surrender of ourselves to the great divine love, and not our desire to control sex and our partners, we will not be satisfied either by sex or by our partners. We will be forever looking outside of ourselves, but never finding, in a state of eternal sexual hunger, with a string of lovers behind us. Because no matter how much sex we may have, we are still as virgins. We are unstirred, and our depths are untouched. This is why I have cheekily called this piece the Second Coming. Because multiple orgasm is <u>one</u> key to our divinity.

I used to be really angry because I could not get into the other realm. I was sad about all my missed experiences of ecstasy. I knew it was possible, but I didn't have knowledge of the key at that time. I didn't really realise that my anger and attachment to peak experiences blocked my having them. Ironically it can demand hard work to let go of your mental dialogue and your judgements enough to just be. But that is what is necessary for ecstatic sexuality. You have to stop trying and just be, in full awareness of the moment, totally aware, because in total presence the ego dies. But also you need not to be hard on yourself for the times you lose that relaxed concentration, because everyone does as thoughts creep in and one attaches to them. The great thing to know and remember is that there will always be more chances as your desire and will to be in ecstatic space increases. It is always there waiting - it's not going to go away. Practice makes perfect. Make time for love!

Chapter 2
How to have ecstatic sex.

Sex is an expression of love, it is an object of love, the physical expression of intimate relationship between people. It is a natural pleasure, created for our healing, relaxation and above all bonding. Therefore it makes sense that we have sex only with those with whom we have a sincere desire to bond. Otherwise we may find that we are linked in negativity with someone whom we do not trust and respect, and this leaves us feeling fearful and degraded. The first condition of ecstatic sexuality is that it be an expression of mutual love.

Sacred sex is a meditative practice, in the sense that one needs to attempt to subdue the activities of the normal mind, in order to experience the fullness of the feelings and sensations that accompany the rhythmic build up of sexual pleasure. Therefore, there is no point in going to lovemaking if one is deeply disturbed by troubles and worries. It is better to have attended to all the necessities in one's life first. If this is impossible, or if spontaneity dictates that there are still ends untied, then one needs to be able to stop worrying and thinking about them. It's impossible to open in holy communion if one's mind is attached to things outside of one's sphere of control. It's a waste of energy.

It is possible to use lovemaking as the focus of concentration, in order to come fully aware and present in the moment. Just to concentrate on the sensation and the feeling in the body, in the heart. If accompanied by an emotion of gratitude for being able to be in the fortunate situation of fusion with another human being, and love for her beloved, a woman can become a conductor and a receptor for the most exquisite exchange of pleasure. It's the most natural thing in the world, very simple, yet we are so full of selfish motive and self opinion that we often miss the simplicity of it.

I suggest that a woman is able to remain focused on the feeling of sex by concentrating on using deep breathing to become aware of the totality of her body. Then at some point, while simply watching her breathing and relaxing deeply, she will become aware of the presence of herself and her lover, joined together in rhythmic motion, as their energies increase and mingle. By concentrating on the physical presence, and aligning themselves with each other in suspended mind dialogue, the lovers open themselves to total telepathic communication, and there will be no need to communicate one's needs through words. In fact there will be no needs, because there is just ecstasy, and in this mindless space there are no longer any needs.

But please don't forget to have fun. There is sometimes an over pre-occupation on the techniques of tantric sex, to the point where the lovers are doing it to be holy. But they have lost the lustiness. It is still a question of having sex to prove something, rather than having sex because you feel like it. The New Age consensus is still on the heroic aspects of sexuality. Having sex for fifty seven hours without coming is a type of conquest, if it's done to measure how spiritual you are.

True tantrists know that every single aspect of life is holy. Sex is one expression of this attitude, which enables us to step through the doorway to other time/space continuums, or in other words to meet God. But it is not the only way, because tantrists are tantric with or without having sex. It's an attitude of mind, which sees God in everything and reveres all life as holy, which takes every experience, painful or pleasurable, as beneficial to one's growth. Nothing in the sphere of one's life is rejected as meaningless, or excluded as an invalid lesson. Tantrists embrace all of life. People who enjoy tantric sex also enjoy communion with all of life's beauty, because the heart is open and therefore experience is full and true.

THE BOOK OF SHABD.

Shabd is the celestial sound - the primal sound current of the universe, which is of a higher frequency than that which we normally attune to. By chanting spiritually charged words or phrases, which are called mantras in Sanskrit, we can raise our frequency to a more subtle level and hence open up our awareness of all things. We increase the radiance of the electro-magnetic energy field that surrounds and protects us, and hence attract beneficial qualities into our lives. Shabd is a way of letting go of earthly connections and connecting to the heavens,through sacred sound. It is one of the tools for the marriage of heaven and earth. The Book of Shabd explores women's experience of religion.

Chapter 1
Woman in Search of the Sacred.

Outside of the cities, in the countryside, it is easier to see the roots of our ancient religions. People are re-discovering sacred sites and practices of old. Of course, they are up against a lot of resistance from the various historical and guardian bodies that control access to the sites. Take for instance Stonehenge, that most famous and mystical temple, constructed with such a sophisticated mixture of esoteric awareness and scientific precision that it appears as a truly New Age phenomenon. Categorised as a site of historical importance, in a land where monotheistic doctrine prevails, any contemporary religious significance of the site is undermined. The fact is, that there are still many people around who would choose to use Stonehenge as a site of worship, in much the same way as they did millennia ago. Moreover there are many others who go there in pursuit of the sacred. The ironic thing about the historical societies that are allocated the preservation and the maintenance of such places is that they are actually draining and depleting the energies of these places by not allowing them to be rightfully used as places of worship. They have assumed that one day the site suddenly lost its meaning. By cordoning off Stonehenge from the public they have turned it into an archaic relic, standing lost and lonely in the emptiness of the Salisbury plain sky. Its emptiness and invalidity is re-inforced by charging tourists from all over the world to troop around the cordoned-off stones, whilst those who would use the site for the purpose it was made, to pray, are denied. It is patriarchal presumption that those of us who wish to re-connect with the source of ancient religions, the ancestral memories of which are in our very blood and bones, are necessarily weirdos and drop-outs. In fact we are simply more able to access what all of us possess, which is the buried genetic memory of the sacred, the spirit of our ancestors. Patriarchal guardians have no respect for those who choose to live alternative definitions of sacred, and crudely block (with ropes and barriers) or even forcefully block (with police cordons), those sites that are claimed by more than one body as being of great value. In their capacity as the preservers of history, they are actually the destroyers of Stonehenge, because they are committing sacrilege - the desecration of the sacred - just as Patriarchs have always done. They have taken a sacred site and allocated it for secular use. Tourists have taken precedence over true worship. But if the site were entrusted to the believers it would surely be maintained and protected with a true energy and gratitude?

It is urgent that we re-discover religion in whatever form or forms this takes. By religion, I mean religiousness, seeing life as sacred. Living life impeccably, without creating more debts and blame, within whichever path inspires us to grow and become liberated from suffering. We need to uncover long buried roots of sacredness and re-define them in new light. Today's Britain is so spiritually starved, so in need of religious regeneration, that the sacred principle of all faiths can offer a part of the golden key to wholeness and happiness. But there is tremendous scope to re-invent religion as well, because there is the urgent cry to revitalise and refresh the sick and exhausted peoples of the world.

The monarchy as head of the monotheistic Church of England is currently bringing the nation into crisis, because it has lost its divine status due to the deceitful and spoilt behaviour of some of its family members. Formerly looked to as demi-Gods, people have at last begun to realise that they are just like themselves, ordinary people, who cheat, lie and manipulate to fulfil their selfish ends. This is sad for the

Royal Family in a way, but more realistic. At the moment many people feel very despondent at this realisation, because they cannot look up to any divine beings and so have lost their faith. There are currently on offer vacancies for spiritual leaders, but they will have to lead impeccable lives. Even so, would we acknowledge them? If Jesus came again, would we be any kinder to him this time? I doubt it. This is why we cannot see, do not believe that there are divine beings walking around the earth today. But they are living protected by layers and layers of outer shell, because we would destroy them with the intensity of our negative energy, if they were to be revealed too soon.

The problem with most Western religions, is that they have fallen into a dogmatic view of life, with the basis that God is separate from us in heaven, while we lowly mortals on earth spend our miserable lives working out how to get back there. This gives us the legitimation to see our lives on earth as unimportant and full of unchangeable suffering, whilst all our striving is to "get out of this place", based on the hope, because we have no real proof, that it will be better next time. Because God is so inaccessible, this type of belief also legitimates hierarchies of holiness, where people set themselves up as closer to God than others. This is the name of Patriarchal religion.

What we are blind to is the fact that both heaven and hell are places within us. Both exist simultaneously, and it is our choice as to which state we subscribe. That is why it is inappropriate to follow religious or spiritual leaders. We must live according to our highest natures. A priest or other religious leader can only temporarily bestow upon us a state of grace. No matter how much we confess, we have to work for this freedom ourselves, by our own actions.

When the Tao, the uninterrupted natural flow of life energy that underlies the cosmos, is personalised, according to the system of the people of that time, the deities will reflect the qualities of worthiness imposed upon them by the human mind. All the descriptions of God that abound in the literature of the various post-Goddess religions share one characteristic - they were all created by man. In the Jewish, Christian (Catholic) and Moslem traditions especially, God is very judgemental of humans. This has lead many people to dump religion as an archaic practice.

Many, especially modern women, can find no place in their lives for such an uninspiring activity, which as anyone with a modicum of intelligence can see, is less about God , than it is about hierarchies and holiness competitions. Patriarchal religions are based on blaming and shaming others. Many modern people are confused, and because of the inadequacy of religion to explain the mystery of life, they have drawn the conclusion there is no God. But because they now have no framework in which to explain the unexplainable, they do not notice it in their lives. There is no explanation for the manifestations of spirit in their lives, so they put everything down to coincidence or accident and miss the joy and humility of witnessing the wonderful workings of the natural mystic law. Therefore they conclude there is no such thing as God and they live in suffering as laws unto themselves, immersed in banality and without a method of regenerating their worn down batteries (time in sacred space recharges our life energies).

There is a God. Or rather there is God in the universe. God is the source and spark of all life. God is pure energy and power. God is what makes the universe go, creation and destruction rolled into one. God is not the creator, so much as the creativity in life. This great power is impartial, unjudgemental yet merciful and infinite. It is merciful because it is love.

Religion however is an organised system of understanding God in human terms, because people cannot incorporate the vastness of this force - God, which is the whole of everything that ever was or is or will be . God is therefore as much in us as outside of us. We are God, but also there is God outside of us. We need to filter and translate this information through a human screen. This is where we have fallen down and missed the point. In this translation, there occurs a corruption of the pure impartial nature of God. Human partiality interferes and creates religions, which then vie with each other for supremacy. Men are possessive of God, but you have no need to possess a force that never ceases and never runs out. But this is the mistake man makes. Because he cannot see this power, he assumes that it is not there, and this is why he has need to create prayer and faith.

The kingdom of God is already here. Christianity, Catholicism, Judaism and Islam fail to recognise this, and so perpetuate people's suffering. The leaders would have them believe that they can never reach heaven until they die. They are being fooled, on a massive scale. In this way, religion is against God. It is dead. But this is false doctrine. By opening our hearts in love, and living truthful lives, we become religious, and can gain enlightenment and experience heaven in our lives. This is living religion, and the only form of religion that is appropriate today.

Because God is said to be outside of the self, in patriarchal religions, man cannot see God. Man cannot either comprehend God, because he does not acknowledge that God is everywhere, and in everything. He finds it so difficult to connect to God, because he does not recognise that the creativity in everything is God. Society has established a system to prevent people from attaining growth and becoming divine themselves, and because man therefore cannot see God, he has to set up an institution - the Church (synagogue, temple, mosque etc) - to represent God, which he believes to be true, but only perpetuates his suffering, because of its denial of the expression of God in everything.

The church is in fact the obstacle which stops man seeing that the true temple is within our own hearts, and the true place of worship begins in the home and not outside of it, and we are the true priests and priestesses of life. Religion without true faith becomes an empty ritual. And since man does not like himself, because of his negative actions and thoughts - an angry one! This is truly idle worship.

God does not demand that we shave our heads (or cover them) to earn his/her grace. God couldn't care less about our heads, God is impartial. God doesn't require women to sit at the back of the temple, or upstairs, or not even allowed inside. God does not require you to damage your children or deny your bodily functions in order to appease him/her/it.

All of these needs of denial are human, and as it appears to me, such self-denigration is based on a dreadful lack of self-worth, and a base belief that God is outside of the self. This is the reason why people need a religion in the first place, because they feel so unworthy of God's love. So the more "devoted"one is, the more worthy one feels, and hence judgements come to be made about one's devotional worth, which becomes like a possession, because it is seen as one's credit score with God.

But God doesn't work according to these principles at all and humans get left behind and lose the point whilst they are busy getting themselves totally bogged down in a fixed system that cannot incorporate the evolution of human consciousness. And this becomes another ground for warring. Let us look for proof of this resistance in the example of the Anglican church, which one might point out is a good deal more advanced in its thinking than many religions.

A historic decision has been reached, that women are to be allowed to ordain as priests. But the debate and fracas that has surrounded the issue has, so we are told, "split the church". Men at war with each other in the name of God is a ridiculous concept, which can only happen, as I said, if people believe God is a resource in short supply who will only bestow upon those who are worthy, by their show of religiousness. Hierarchies are the order of the day in religions.

But a true religion is, or should be, a tool for increasing our self-worth. It then becomes a force for unification, pleasure and the end of all suffering.

God never runs out, and self-worth, for both males and females, can only come from one's own faith in oneself, based on righteousness. We are all manifestations of God, in a sense, we are all a piece of God, and this makes us Gods and Goddesses in our own right. We have the power to be good or not good, but we will have to live with the consequences of the causes we make in our lives. These causes will accumulate, and work from deep within our lives to create our circumstances. We all have preconditioned responses. These determine how we live our lives and whether or not we can be happy. This is known in Eastern philosophies as karma, and it is why we, as light beings, come to inhabit the earth in the first place. Those of us who have no karma do not incarnate, and those of us who have less, like Jesus, come to teach us all. Our ultimate goal is to uncondition our responses, so that we stop creating karma, and become happy.

It is precisely in changing and erasing our karma that we build self-worth. Because this is us doing God's work on Earth, and it is what we are here for. To get fixed in and by religion makes not a jot of impact upon God, if we do not believe in ourselves.

The way to God, is, in all cases, in us changing our karma - changing our suffering into joy, changing our pain into pleasure. Changing the causes we make in this life and all past and future lives.

As I see it, our suffering, which is what religions are

based on (we white western peoples have never forgiven ourselves for destroying Jesus), our self punishment, and self-flagellation, our confession and atonement, all of these gestures of self-disapproval may make us feel better. But God doesn't need them at all. God doesn't need anything from us at all. God just is, whether we see God or not. What God does do is to grant us the free will to make the choices to achieve some growth, some personal evolution, which is the sign that we have connected to God and listened to the teachings as they have manifested through our spirits, and beckoned our consciousness. In this human life, we have a hard time accepting that each human being has the god-given right to experience their own karma, whether we like it or not.

Whether or not we truly change our behaviour in this world, towards each other and towards the planet we inhabit, our environment, makes not a jot of difference to God. This unseen power will still be doing its work regardless, of creating, supporting and destroying life. We can destroy the Earth, but we cannot destroy God.

God is not outside ourselves. We are God. Yet we have built temples and shrines. But God resides in the temples of our hearts and it is our power to feel good or bad, which everyone can have - rich or poor, male or female, able or disabled. Every one of us has a direct link to God, whose messages will come through our own intuition and need not be translated by a priest, medium or supposed more holy person than oneself. Everyone, whatever their social status, has a chance to go through the door to unfoldment. Everyone has their own personal karma. Everyone can change their life for the better, for the saner, for the happier. There are no exclusions. This is God's law. God's message is always clear and simple. Do your work, erase your karma and evolve. You have chosen to incarnate to aid your soul's development. Therefore become who you truly are!

*The worship of the female divine is the honouring of
ourselves.*

Do we need to worship God?

I believe that worship, in the sense of paying respect to,
divine descriptions of life, is an important part of our unfolding consciousness. By honouring and worshipping images or
figures of saintly qualities, we invoke those qualities in our
lives. We are therefore worshipping ourselves, in the sense
that we are calling up our own divine qualities. We are
bridging the separation between ourselves and God. It's not
that there is any separation, but we have come to believe that
there is, therefore we have to recover our connection to the
divine.

Therefore it doesn't much matter which divine representation we choose, since it is only a representation of the
nameless and unimaginable power of the creator, sustainer
and destroyer, who is of course neither male nor female, but
contains the wholeness of both energies. It is a matter of personal taste and vibration, to which manifestation of spirit one
prays. Nevertheless a woman who is rapidly developing
spiritually needs to make connection with female qualities of
divinity.

Much of the traditional imagery surrounding female
Goddesses emphasises their nurturing and protective powers. Mother Goddesses are revered by male and female
devotees in Hinduism. The tremendous compassion of the
divine mother as she heals the flock of wounded children
who pass before her to receive her blessing is awesome in its
emotional power. The divine mother sustains and loves her
children sincerely and unconditionally and provides one
model of a Goddess for us to worship.

However, apart from the figure of the Mother Goddess,

no other female aspect of the deity is widely worshipped today. The point about the mother Goddess is that we were all born from women, so the honouring of one's mother is a natural spiritual step for those who are embarking upon the spiritual path. However what is not so prevalent is the worship of qualities that surround woman as a sexual being. Especially when female sexuality is seen as not linked with destruction. For instance Kali, the great Goddess of India, fills people with fear, as she is associated with death and destruction as she dances on Shiva. But the death is really only the destruction of Maya - illusion - beyond which is enlightenment.

The sexual healing power of women is not accorded in most faiths, and is shunned in the notion of the uncleanliness of woman and the strong belief in the need to renounce a sexual life in order to gain God's grace.

This belief causes untold pain and hardship to women who are both sexual and spiritual, because there are few schools of thought that recognise and even honour female sexuality as the powerful healing force that it truly can be. But there is a vast body of sacred erotica that women need to uncover and re-live, because it is our heritage and our path forwards to living a spirituality that does not exclude central parts of ourselves as have all patriarchal modes of worship.

There is nothing wrong with giving devotion to the male aspects of God-as father, as son, and as lover. In fact it's a necessary component of a balanced spiritual life. However the over worshipping of the male aspects of the deity have not stopped this world from being brought to the brink of extinction and have not yet relieved humanity of suffering. Therefore we have not yet found the answer in the scores of religions and cults that only or predominantly worship God in his male form.

Chapter 2
Sacred Silence, Sacred Sound.

The Buddhist-Feminist path.

Buddhism teaches us very firmly, and provides us with the empirical proof, that we can turn this life into joy, by changing our negative karma. Karma refers to the accumulation of causes one makes for one's life, by one's thoughts, behaviour and attitude. The onus is very much on the power of the self, because one starts to take responsibility for creating one's own life circumstances. Buddhism is a tremendously poetic and beautiful philosophy which can help us to cultivate the qualities of wisdom, compassion and calmness.

However, within Buddhism there are so many different strands and sects, so many different religions even. In fact there is not even one Buddha, although we tend to think of the father of Buddhism as Shakyamuni Buddha, the one who renounced his princely life to live as a mendicant, the one who gained enlightenment under the Bodhi tree. But although Buddhists pay their allegiance to the Buddha, they do not worship him as a god. He is seen more as the teacher, the transmitter of wisdom and knowledge. The relationship with him is one of respect rather than worship.

Buddhism encompasses a vast and evolving philosophy (it is not considered to be a religion) that has spanned across the whole of the Orient and is now firmly implanted in the West. Is it appropriate for feminists today to practice Buddhism? Because Buddhism is a therapeutic practice, in which we open ourselves to the development of our in-built Buddha nature, leading to enlightenment, or absolute freedom from suffering, I do not believe that it compromises feminists.

We must remember that the forefathers of Buddhism, Shakyamuni and his cronies, did not at first believe that a woman or a lay person could become enlightened. This was only renounced at the end of the Buddha's life. But the Sutras, or doctrines of knowledge upon which the practice is based, other than the Lotus Sutra, were formulated before this thinking about women had been changed. So in a sense, Buddhist women need to be sure that they are not buying into their own diminishment in the study materials they are covering.

There are so many schools of thought within Buddhist philosophy, which has branched out all over the world. The traditional Buddhism, (Hinayana - Theravada) which is still practiced in Sri Lanka and parts of S.E. Asia is an essentially monastic, celibate and rigorous path to individual enlightenment - Nirvana. It involves practicing penances and austerities to efface the ego, and gain the Buddha's grace. It is therefore a God-fearing path to enlightenment, which as such is not going to lead a woman to freedom. Unless of course within the discipline of monastic life she can gain enough clarity to become free of the fixedness.

Only with the advent of Mahayana Buddhism came the acceptance and acknowledgement that all people, not just monks and priests, could become enlightened. This opened the doors of the faith to women. The roots of Mahayana Buddhism are woman-centred. Tantric Tibetan Buddhism derives from Indian matristic cultures. Tantra is symbolised by the union of Shiva and Shakti, as male and female energies merge into each other.

The Chanting Priestess.

For those of us who do not feel comfortable with the idea of divinity as present in emptiness as some forms of

Buddhist meditation practice emphasise, there are other forms of meditation practice that involve visualisation and devotion to the female Buddhas. Actually the divine is both formless and with form. So it is perfectly acceptable to practice both methods of form and formlessness in the search for the energy of the sacred. There is nothing incongruous or confusing in meditating on emptiness and then giving devotional worship to a divine being. Both feel good and lead to the development of insight and love. As long as we are aware that there is no duality. As eclectic Buddhists, and feminists, we reserve the right to draw upon techniques from all practices as tools to self-development.

Many teachings of all faiths stress the practice of repeating the holy names of God, or divine beings, in the form of mantras. A mantra is a sacred mystic syllable, word or phrase chanted to invoke God, gods or god-like qualities. Repetitively recited it is known as Japa. Although one starts from the premise of duality, in that God is seen as outside of oneself, the repeated chanting of the sacred name eventually overcomes the duality, and the chanter becomes one with God.

This is the practice of many Hindu aspects of worship, such as the Hare Krishna. I have more fully elaborated this later on in this book. The point of this section is to show you how to begin to practice Japa, because it is so beautiful to do so.

Once Japa is established one can practice it anywhere, and this is the simplicity and beauty of the practice. You are literally growing your love for God. Hence you are also growing your love for yourself. So you require nothing other than your desire to become one with the source of your life. Japa is particularly good if you have a family, because you can still chant and get on with things.

However, I would recommend establishing a sacred

space in which to worship, because then you can set up an altar, with the object of your worship, which will help you to intensify the strength of your practice.

Prajnaparamita was the Buddhist Goddess whose teachings are the foundation of Mahayana Buddhism. The Boddhisattvas of Mahayana Buddhism are themselves liberated beings, but have taken the vow to forego the entry into the state of Nirvana while suffering still exists among humanity. The main function of the Boddhisattvas (ones who are wise and compassionate), is to bring salvation to others. Amongst these saviours of humanity, we women can look to the ministrations of the Goddess Tara, as the embodiment of female wholeness in divinity.

Green Tara

Tara is said to be the saviouress, who leads humanity from suffering to enlightenment. She is a Boddhisattva and fully enlightened Buddha (awakened one), a Tantric deity, who transmits her wisdom, energy and power through her being, in the eroticism of her sexuality as well as in everyday life. She is closely connected to nature and earth, to animals and plants as well as people. Thus she is a very earthy, earthly Goddess, full of love and lust for life, at the same time aware of the suffering of all her people and the need to stay back and help them across the ocean of suffering. In this way Tara is the mother of all the people, but also their lover, as she passes on the knowledge of the sacredness and joy of sex.

The mantra to invoke Tara is **Om Tare Tuttare Ture Swaha.**

By chanting with devotion to the Goddess Tara one can be assured of speedy deliverance from suffering. Women who chant devotedly to her bring forth their Tara qualities, healing and empowering their sacred feminine energies.

Ecstatica

Nam-Myoho-Renge-Kyo (The Buddhism of the Latter Day of the Law).

Still on the theme that all beings can continually evolve through repeating the chosen sacred name, the dynamic Buddhism of Nichiren Daishonin redresses the dogmatism that was inherent in earlier teachings. He proclaimed chanting Nam-Myoho-Renge-Kyo, which is the title of the Lotus Sutra (Devotion to the Sutra of the Perfect Law of the Lotus). Chanting this sacred mantra is proven to be a very powerful practice, that has the potential for completely healing the damaged hearts of people and raising the level of humanity to the heart chakra. The word Myo also means to open. The regular, repeated chanting of the phrase, the theory being that all the aspects of the Sutra are contained within its title, confers the qualities of Buddahood upon the devotee. The Buddhism of Nichiren Daishonin is the most modern form of the religion, which sees the potential of Buddhahood at the core of every individual, man or woman.

By putting our faith in the mystic law of Nam-Myoho-Renge-Kyo we are assured of the eventual unfolding of our higher self (Buddhahood), which although it may not be always apparent, is nevertheless like the sun behind the clouds, always present. By chanting sincerely, we align ourselves with the mystic law and tap into our own Buddha natures, thereby creating the causes to change our karma and hence the quality of our lives in this incarnation, and all future lives and one might even add the karma of past lives. We can even chant for the dead, to change their karma too. It is a profoundly dynamic tool for changing our consciousness and a moving force. In fact, one might even add, while chanting, it feels like you are whipping up the horses that pull your vehicle, and getting them to go full speed ahead with your life. All evidence points to the fact that people who chant are able to take control of their lives and transform their chaos into some order, or as the faith says, by chanting Nam-Myoho-Renge-Kyo, one is able to change the poisons of anger, greed and ignorance into medicine.

Chanting provides us with a mirror by which we are able to reflect and see our life condition. The problems do not go away, in fact it may even seem quite the opposite when one starts to chant, but one is given the energy and protection to confront and challenge them. By this resolve to deal with obstacles and hindrances that arise, one can grow in will and personal power.

The supreme object of worship in this type of Buddhism is not a person, but a sacred scroll - the impartial Gohonzon, representing the relationship between humans and the mystic law. The Gohonzon is the central object of worship - Gohonzon means object worthy of respect and honour. The Gohonzon is a scroll in the form of a mandala, inscribed with Chinese characters that is derived from the original Dai Gohonzon inscribed in Japan in 1279. A wood block print copy of the original is issued to lay members of the association of Nichiren Buddhists when they participate in a membership ceremony. This is obviously an emotional and momentous occasion for a woman Buddhist. However, where there is true faith, a physical representation of that is only a symbol of one's commitment. If the Buddha/God is not in one's heart, then God is nowhere.

Nichiren Daishonin's Buddhism is a particularly applicable spiritual tool for women who are self-motivated, but whose lives tend to be chaotic and out of control. It does not involve conforming to any specific lifestyle, because by realising one's Buddha nature, one will make correct choices, so it demands nothing of an individual in the way of sacrifice, or renunciation. It is crucial that women change their negative karma based on fear and self-worthlessness. As one's practice becomes more assured and one's faith deepens, the Buddha qualities of wisdom and compassion naturally develop. By chanting, answers to one's problems spontaneously arise. This is because we are tapping into our intuitive sense. Touching the place inside ourselves from where our wisdom stems. It is like we become the oracle at Delphi - the woman who channels knowledge directly from spirit. One is able to reach awareness of one's psychological patterns. Painful though this may be, it is a thousand times better than living in the abject state of shut-down that is the alternative to naming one's faulty programming or karma.

There is no doubt that Nam-Myoho-Renge-Kyo is beautiful for women to practice, because there is no master, and a woman can be her own priestess. As she grows, so does her fortune. It is highly intelligent and very practical. In fact Nichiren Daishonin's Buddhism is said in the Sutras to be the only type of Buddhism that is applicable for the Latter Day of the Law, which is the period beginning 2000 years after the death of Shakyamuni Buddha, when his teachings will lose their power and the true teacher is going to appear to lead all people to enlightenment. It is also believed to be the only type of Buddhism that women can participate in on an equal basis with men.

However despite the obvious wisdom of practicing this Buddhism, the proof of one's faith can only lie in the increased happiness one makes in one's life. Nichiren Daishonin declared the sacred law of Nam-Myoho-Renge-Kyo amidst tumultuous opposition. He was even sentenced to exile and almost executed for his work, nevertheless he persisted in his faith. His life is an example of faith.

What was once just confined to Japan, Nam-Myoho-Renge-Kyo now has millions of believers worldwide and the number is still growing. It took the atomic bomb, the feminist movement, the flower power generation and other revolutions in consciousness that have occurred this century, for the seeds of this religion to propagate in the West. To ensure that the practice remains dynamic depends upon that whatever directives we receive from truly uncovering our Buddhahood are incorporable into our lives. If the religion becomes static then we will grow beyond it. This is what tends to happen to women who practice existing, organised religion in our society. As the women grow in independence and spirit, so they outgrow the other members of their faith who remain fearful, judgemental and dogma-bound. In other words as they quote aspects of the fixed faith, they are in fact lacking in true faith. They are God-fearing and woman mistrusting. But God-fearing has no place in any religion that is appropriate for feminists.

Nichiren's Buddhism is so broad in its scope and compassion, that there is no one whom it cannot incorporate, providing it is practiced in its purity and essence. Therefore, as long as Buddhahood, and not dogma, determines life choices, the movement will continue to spiral towards its goal of creating world happiness, by starting with Buddhist believers, who as they grow in depth are able to begin to see outside of themselves, towards transforming the pain of others. This is the mission for Kosen Rufu - to widely spread and propagate Buddhism. They are the Boddhisattvas of the Earth. Those who are independent in their faith will nevertheless create benefits for others. From the point of one's Buddha nature, one always does what is true and right. Therefore there is no God to fear. One trusts implicitly in one's own wisest voice, accessed in the space of one's own Buddha nature. From the point of view of the true root of the practice, there is nothing a woman of impeccability could do that could be un-Buddhist.

There is no doubt that this past half century has seen a fundamental change in our wiring, so to speak and we have begun a huge shift in human awareness. Chanting Nam-Myoho-Renge-Kyo has its part in this growth, and indeed it is precisely why the practice has spread in the West. Nam-Myoho-Renge-Kyo is a valid and powerful tool for changing one's consciousness and hence one's karma.

However I believe women of integrity need have no fixed religion, yet can still be religious. I think they may have a spiritual practice that is established or one that is quite unique. It may remain the same or it may change and adapt itself, according to the nature of the day, the season, her commitments, her lifestyle or whatever consideration. We have to be sure that we do what is appropriate for us, and keep reaffirming its validity. It is important in the matter of feminist spirituality to avoid dogmatism. For a feminist, truly her life must be her religion. The only judge of a woman's spirituality is her own self-worth. The only thing that matters is that her religion, if she has one, increases her well-being and her integrity. That it represents some form of personal growth and self-empowerment, or she can make it do so, and that above all it opens up her creativity and her heart to the compassion and love that is the nature of creation. In other words whatever she chooses to do to tap into the source is fine.

Often however, within religious orders and groups, we confuse spirituality with self-effacement. We think that to be truly humble, means asserting no individuality, no uniqueness, no lust for life. But if we lack self-worth, we will be unable to trust our own judgements, unable to distinguish between a correct action and an incorrect one. So we will have to stick by the rule book. This is what one so often comes across in religious movements - the assumption that everyone is equally unworthy and sinful when left to their own devices. So much so, that even what set out as an undogmatic philosophy, nevertheless becomes one. This is the trouble with patriarchal religions. However there is always something to be gained from every situation, in terms of the growth it can afford us by causing us to examine our assumptions about life.

If women Buddhists feel belittled by their peers, then they are best advised to practice home alone according to their intuition, whilst seeking out and connecting to other similarly inspired women. Women who feel mature enough, wise enough and free enough to pray and chant together and evolve their practice, not according to dogma, but in line with their own or a respected teacher's guidelines. That is what a spiritual teacher should be. Not a definitive master, or guru, but a sacred guide, who can help sincere seekers, not disciples or followers, to become whole again. Buddhism teaches us to be unjudgemental of others. We must respect that everyone has free will, and that we can never hope to fully understand the world from the perspective of another's karma. All we can do is to support each other in faith.

Doing Daimoku (chanting Nam-Myoho-Renge-Kyo repeatedly) is a good way to prepare the mind for really deep meditation. Nam-Myoho-Renge-Kyo is an aid to concentration to enable deep connection with 'the source' to occur. It is therefore a shamanic tool. SGI (Sokka Gakkai International - the Buddhist society for the creation of value through peace, education and culture) guidelines suggest that the eyes be kept open and fixed on the Gohonzon, the supreme object of worship, representing our Buddha nature. Gohonzon is like a mirror of our own inner reality. The Gohonzon was inscribed as the highest life state of Nichiren Daishonin. By chanting to the Gohonzon, we are therefore invoking our own highest life state.

So many of us are desperately seeking, casting about, clutching at straws, trying to find the golden key to our problems that will make us feel better. We have not yet realised that we will only be able to find the answers deep inside ourselves. For that is where the problems lie. We think it to be terribly difficult to connect to our true selves, but really the answer is simple. You just have to let go. Surrender yourself to the infinite. Ask and you shall be given. Nam-Myoho-Renge-Kyo is just one of the tools that can make you happy.

I am not saying that we can overcome all oppression. There will be suffering while there is duality in life on earth. But what chanting does is to make us aware that we have a choice of how to react to a situation, as well as the chance to then change the causes we make for the future. There is a huge spin off effect that is the power we create by positive thought and visualisation. By chanting to reveal our Buddha natures, we encourage all those around us to connect with us from their own Buddha natures. They simply cannot resist the power of this, because it is the truth of the mystic law at work. Support is given to the power of one's own psychic energy in creating the world. This is in total contrast to the patriarchal constraint that we do not venture beyond the first world, outer shell of materialism, and in fact even denies that there is anything beyond this outer, visible reality.

Chanting is a brilliant tool for overcoming addictions, because addictions to external stimuli are ways to avoid living with the reality of one's true nature, devoid of any artificially aided states of being. Women who are, or have been addicted to substances that alter their consciousness might have a hard time when they decide to give up the substance because it is no longer furthering their development to create false euphoria, rather than hang out for true Buddhahood. So this is the kind of uncomfortable situation that chanting consistently can truly help us to get through. Because by experiencing her Buddhahood through chanting and indeed affirming that it is there, just underneath her surface, a woman can gain the strength and courage to overcome her addictions. It is a matter of summoning true faith, which is the faith to believe that one is indeed a Buddha, who needs nothing other than her own natural resources to achieve absolute freedom from all suffering. The good thing about Nam-Myoho-Renge-Kyo is that it is a well organised and incredibly worldwide spread practice. There are members everywhere, so if you need support and consistency to begin with to keep up your momentum, you will find their wisdom encouraging.

Even those of us who are not addicted to substances, are nevertheless addicted to negative behaviour patterns. We are hooked on being weak in certain situations, - with men, with our parents, with people whom we fear, - and adept only at burying our emotions, which we hide not only from others, but also from ourselves. Many of us are adepts at working our wills through manipulation, rather than direct confrontation, and this type of pattern is so deeply entrenched that we may have a hard time even recognising it, let alone changing it. The law of Nam-Myoho-Renge-Kyo will help you to recognise your emotional patterns and also give you the courage to face up to them and to name them and thus there will come a time when the pain of being a liar and a cheat will no longer haunt our lives.

If your life is in chaos, out of your control, and you feel that others are to blame for your situation, or if you simply feel your life is not working well enough for you, and that includes most of us, and you have no religious faith nor a spiritual path, then I would advise you to start to sincerely chant Nam-Myoho-Renge-Kyo. Trust! Let the chanting take you where it will.

Chapter 3
Becoming A Feminist Yogi.

Still looking to the East for esoteric wisdom, we come to the spiritual body of knowledge, from the sub-continent of India, that is known as Yoga. The sheer scope and size of sacred teachings that originate there means that they can hardly afford to be ignored. Again, it was the rapid acceleration in consciousness that characterised the sixties, that opened and attracted us to the mystical nature of many of the Yogic teachings. Whilst once doing Yoga was thought to be an eccentric and alternative thing, it is now so commonplace that it can be found on the syllabus of every local education authority college.

The benefits of Yoga are well documented. It has generally come to mean the system of practicing various bodily postures (asanas), mental exercises (meditations) and breathing techniques (pranayama), to achieve improved health and overall well-being. However Yoga actually means union. It is both a method and ultimately a state of being, wherein an individual's consciousness can become united with the supreme consciousness - the impartial, undifferentiated source of all life - God. Such a state is more commonly called enlightenment.

This latter realisation of the power of Yoga, is only likely to become comprehensible and attainable by those individuals who commit themselves to Yoga as a way of life. However there is no saint without a sinner's past, and it is as good a way as any to start Yoga at evening class, except that the sacredness of the practice tends to be hard to summon up under the lights and smells of the average local education college.

Even the simplest practice of Yoga exercises can bring amazing benefits to the health and balance in one's life. But it is worth stressing that Yoga is in fact a vast art and an exact science for spiritual liberation, should the path call to you. Nevertheless, as a woman who is intent on following the path of Yoga, it is important to question and to be empowered to re-define any aspects of the philosophy and practice that are by virtue of their history or partiality, inapplicable to our lives as modern, feminist women.

Many of us who come to Yoga are educated women, who have studied widespread philosophies. We know about different religions and belief systems across many cultures, both historically and today. Some of us may likely have been born into a family practicing or subscribing to a religious dogma. We may have spent our childhood years being indoctrinated with the religion of our families. This might have determined the type and nature of education we received and even the social life that we were allowed. In rejection of our birth religion, but nevertheless continuing the search for the sacred, we may have come to believe in another religion, seemingly more "spiritual" than the original one we were granted. We may have rejected the religion of our forebears as patriarchal, particularly if it was a monotheistic Judaeo-Christian one, and yet embraced another less obviously patriarchal one, such as Hinduism, Sikhism or Buddhism. The Eastern faiths, whilst they contain much within their bounds which is dogmatic and oppressive to women, particularly by their failure to give voice to women's pain, can nevertheless offer the seeds of "enlightenment"to feminists who seek spiritual growth.

Life is at optimum health where male and female balance and complement each other, may one even say adore each other. But there is an over-emphasis on the worship of the father that is common to most religions, Eastern and Western alike, that prevents religions from being truly powerful forces for change. Religions stay put in the dark ages, their followers practice penances and other affirmations of self-worthlessness and leave true spiritual aspirants having been led to the truth, yet unable to practice it within the bounds of their faith, because their self-reliance will be mistrusted.

Becoming a holy woman is crucial to our survival, but this does not imply a male defined spirituality. Holy in its original sense means to be whole. We know it when we feel it. It is in depth connection, which is characterised by ecstasy. It is being in love, although with no one in particular. Sexy can be holy, if sexiness is a manifestation of our connection with ourselves, with each other and with our source. But too many religions, both eastern and western, have problems with bodily experiences, rejecting them as non-spiritual. In effect this view is very life denying and particularly prejudiced against women who spend much of their natural lives immersed in bodily experiences.

Eating, making love, giving birth, are all sacred experiences. The body is there to be embraced, not rejected. It makes no sense at all to reject certain of our experiences and does not respect our creation. Religions that practice renunciation of pleasurable (or potentially pleasurable) human experience deny our birthright and are "playing God" themselves from the point of their fears and insecurities.

This sacrifice of pleaure is not the truth. Many religious aspirants who choose to marry God are in fact denying God/the Goddess, by rejecting the possibility of earthly fusion and love with another human being. In my view the true priests and priestesses of humanity are those who can and do bond in deep ecstatic communion with each other. This is not to say that a sole practitioner cannot be holy, but that there is no need to be celibate to be so. If one chooses celibacy because one's relations with the opposite sex are negative and diminish one's self-worth, then the truly religious thing to do is to confront these tendencies through relationship and to change them.

The mistaken belief that God is male, and that he inhabits the sky, has turned religious seekers away from seeing the sacredness of material earthly life, into which rejection have been lumped the experiences and attributes of women. This mistaken assumption pervades all religions and it is the task of the religious feminist to decode the basic information and see if there is any way we can extract the truth from the core of our religion. If we cannot do this, then the religion is invalid for us. However I believe that there is, at the heart of every faith, an unchanging truth, a vision of grace beyond words that exhorts us to do everything in our power to bring that vision into our lives. This is what we need to remember in our spiritual practice. We must bring the real God back to religion.

It is with this in mind that I look to the philosophy and science of Yoga to provide us with the tools to enhance our lives.

In traditional cultures, historically, a Yoga student would follow one of the six main different paths of Yoga to enlightenment. The different types of Yoga offered different methods of attaining the goal of self-realisation, depending upon the nature of the aspirant and the teaching of the chosen Guru.

A spiritual feminist practicing Yoga today needs to look for the universal truth at the heart of Yoga philosophy. If she has a teacher, then that person should be her guide to sacred consciousness, who can lead her to her own highest potential. But it is she who must do the work, not the teacher. There are so many followers and devotees of gurus and masters. But eventually they too should become inspired leaders if the teacher is genuine and correct. No honest teachers want to hold power over their students, and they would be delighted to see their students growth and liberation. Only a person with true humility can become spiritually liberated.

I believe that in order to avail herself of the impartial truth, which is the working of the natural law, a woman should best practice all the methods of Yoga, freed from their patriarchal emphasis, at one and the same time, thus creating a new form of woman-centred Yoga which is non competitive and personally empowering. In this way, feminist Yoga is not only a practical possibility, it also becomes a dynamic and rapidly life changing life-work.

The most commonly encountered form of Yoga in the West today is known as **Hatha Yoga.** It involves controlling the body and bodily functions as a means of stilling the mind. This is done through the practice of Asanas (postures) which are held steady and Pranayama (the control and regulation of the breath).

Breathing is a feminist issue.

We are all subject to the quality of air that our environment, both locally and globally, affords us. Those of us who live in the city have to endure pollution. Ghastly sick-making fumes and noise are a way of life. Unleaded petrol and catalytic converters are the tip of the iceberg. They do not address the real problem, which concerns the volume of traffic and the amount of unecessary travel that we indulge in. Capital cities are 24-hour thinking machines that offer no respite from the over-intensive concentration of peoples' vibrations. Sundays in the city can be like a breath of heaven as a small amount of regeneration occurs. Nevertheless it is impossible to achieve any depth of healing in meditation within a large city, because there is no stillness. Silence heals. Without immersing ourselves in the powerful quality of silence we can find it hard to turn off our internal dialogues,

198

and hence become anxious and neurotic. Our health is at risk in the cities of the world; however, we find we are forced to be there (or believe we are) in order to secure enough income to survive. We cannot all exit the cities at this time, and anyway many areas of the countryside are toxic. But we do need to structure our lives so that we can have frequent access to wild and sacred spaces, where we can re-charge our worn down batteries and in the silence of these places, find the inspiration to follow our destinies.

This is why we should be prepared to assure that we are doing our upmost to secure the quality of air for ourselves and our families, by the way in which we treat our air. Many so called feminists smoke, whether due to stress or habit. However in my view a feminist would never commit a will-fully life destroying act, either for herself or towards another. Despite the difficulty involved in breaking the negative patterns of a lifetime, she will muster the will to stop smoking, because the passion of her commitment to the environment is greater than her need to fill in her own empty space with a toxic emotional crutch like cigarettes or alcohol.

We must learn how to breathe because, although we do it automatically, we do not do it consciously and as such we do not breathe correctly. Most of us have forgotten how to breathe. The interesting thing about breathing is, the more oxygen you take in, the less negative thought you hang onto, and breathing helps us to release negative patterns and imprints that we have been holding onto, perhaps even from birth. In fact this is the basis of the Art of Rebirthing.

Of course there is a time and place for proper deep breathing, and if you should be so unfortunate as to be walking down 5th avenue, the Champs Elysees or Oxford St, or driving around the Los Angeles freeway or around the M 25, then it is obviously going to be more dangerous to breathe deeply than not. But time should be set aside daily to practice proper breathing exercises until such control becomes second nature.

Breath is magical. It is the key to life. It is the first thing we do once we emerge from our mothers' wombs. Before sucking even we breathe. Long, deep breathing is so powerful that it can restructure our bodies at the cellular level. It changes our rhythm and helps us to adapt to the rhythm of life which pulses through everything.

Hatha Yoga Asanas combined with deep abdominal breathing will help you to let go of tension and fear. They are good for regular practice. Many of them have animal names as they are said to bear resemblance to the shape or nature of the creature they invoke. For example Cobra, which is the uncurling of the spine, is said to awaken the Serpent Goddess (or Kundalini Energy), the Cat and the Dog refer to different ways of stretching the spine, whereas Cat/Cow indicates a technique where one shifts from one spinal stretch into another by arching the back, neck and head.

Some of the standard Yoga texts depict men arranged in near impossible positions. It is not necessary to become a contortionist, and practicing Yoga asanas as a matter of competition either with oneself or others, is not the point. Every body is different. Some are more flexible or more physically tuned than others. The whole idea is to improve and increase one's own health, vitality and longevity, which is of course also, a feminist pre-requisite.

Raja Yoga is the science/art of mental control. It incorporates Hatha Yoga Asanas, which it advances upon, as well as Pranayama (yogic breathing) and meditation. But it also demands the acceptance of certain "moral" principles aimed at overcoming human beings baser natures. These are non-violence (towards animals as well), truthfulness, non-stealing, moderation in all things and non-attachment to material things. Raja Yoga aims to "conquer" the mind and develop its constructive powers, by controlling the thought waves that would otherwise control us. The aphorisms (sayings) of Patanjali, an Indian sage from over 1500 years ago, form the basis of the teachings of Raja Yoga, which is known as the Royal path, and considered to be one of the most difficult of all Yoga paths.

How then can this ancient philosophy help feminist spiritual seekers today?

To answer this question we need to look in more detail at the nature of the thought waves that are the stem of our thoughts.

Our minds are like computers. First of all receptive (original), then the system for receiving and processing data has to be installed (patriarchy), then finally we can run the programmes (our ego). However, the beauty of the system is that it can be re-wired to accept new information. This is the task I and many of my sisters are currently totally immersed in. There is nothing more worth doing, because it is the sacred work that is going to re-balance the Earth. It is our responsibility to face and transform ourselves, with compassion and support from others, because we are the recipients of the knowledge that can save all humanity from suffering. In other words, we have been informed from the highest sources of our own divinity, of the joyful news that Armageddon is not on the cosmic schedule, as previously prophesied by some of the gloomier prophets of the past, and that in fact we are to work for a happier era. This means on the one hand that we can all breathe a sigh of relief and relax, and on the other we must work full-tilt to usher in this post-patriarchal reality. This affords us the task of being both calm and relaxed, yet always ready to fight for the truth. In other words peaceful warriors.

Yoga offers us the technology to become both of these qualities. To attain both peace of mind (meditation) and strength of spirit and endurance (asanas). It allows us to work dynamically and purposefully and yet maintain our balance. Without such technology we would perhaps be in

201

danger of burn-out as so many feminists are today, unable to counteract their rightful rage at the pain they see around them.

By bringing the quality of silence into our lives, through meditation, we allow a pause in the programmes that we are running, to see our own manner of operating. We have, without exception, all been programmed by the patriarchal consensus view of reality. Hence our programmes fall into line with acceptable models for little girls within the limits of this system. Many of us have suffered developmental arrests at some point in our early lives due to lack of parental maturity and feedback, and we have become stuck in the programme, playing out our own particular patriarchal script. It doesn't get us what we really need which is compassionate, unconditional love, but nevertheless it is all we know how to do to get any feedback at all, so we continue to do it. It is one thing in a child, but a grown woman having tantrums, or wheedling her way around men or whatever, is no longer appropriate.

There are endless variations of de-powered female scripts (negative female karma), that we play out as our egos. There is the little girl who can't get daddy's or mummy's attention and so learns ways (dramatic) of bringing attention to herself; the overly responsible little girl with pathetic parents, who dare not be a child or enjoy herself for fear her parents will come to harm; the monstrous little girl who can do no wrong in her parents' eyes, or maybe just in daddy's eyes, making mummy jealous and manipulating to split her parents and so on. Do any of these habitual, unconscious patterns sound familiar? Of course they do, because we are none of us exempt from the woman-hating basis from which all of our thinking derives. So our thoughts, based on these programmes, rise up, and until we have cleared the negative belief at their root, they will continue to pull our emotions through the range of self-destructive patterns, namely fear, anger and sadness, all of which freeze us from action - other than destructive action - and which cripple and psychically maim us, cutting us off from ourselves and others, making bonding with others on an emotional basis and in love, an impossibility. Our female programmes contain layers upon layers of trickery, whereby we fool ourselves and others, because the point is we are set up to fail. So even before we have started out, we are not going to succeed, because failure is in-built in the programme. But remember, they are just programmes, they are not the real you, whose nature is pure and untarnished(original).

Raja Yoga, like chanting Nam-Myoho-Renge-Kyo, provides us with the technology to become aware of our inner motivation, as thoughts and feelings that we had not been conscious of begin to work themselves out as we relax more and more. This new awareness of how we have been really functioning gives us the choice to interrupt those sequences, to create a small pause into which we can feed new information, based upon our unfolding, on the validity of who we are now and who we sincerely want to become, and not just bound by how we habitually view life. Through certain exercises and proper breath, we stimulate our love energy as we open ourselves to the divine flow, the source of all life that pulses through the universe, but because the psychic baggage we carry is so heavy, we normally cannot tune into it. The practice of these techniques allows us to shed this baggage and hence to become open to the timeless wisdom at the heart of all life.

If and when we really monitor our thought patterns, to stalk ourselves and face up to the truth of our intent, however painful, then and only then, can we begin to see the nature of patriarchal dialogue as it manifests in what some might like to call our individuality. In fact, until we have carried out this sacred work of de-programming the patriarchal ideology from our own computers, we are not individuals at all, but more like patriarchal robots, automatons who cannot act according to free will. In fact we have not at this stage yet freed our will.

Sometimes women do break free of these restrictions. In fact the papers are full of stories of women who have broken beyond the bounds of their programming. But the overwhelming emphasis is on women who just snap and do dreadful and destructive things like go mad or kill people or themselves. This again of course reflects our patriarchal emphasis. How many accounts do we equally hear of women who have broken through and beyond their programming - the witches and female sorcerers, seers and shamans, who are at this minute striving to free themselves of their conditioning in order to help and heal themselves and others?

This is why the knowledge from Raja Yoga can be a useful tool to help us to break out of our chains. Because it can offer us the ability to observe and hence come to know our own programmes (ego). Watching and unjudgementally recording as they arise, we can eventually come to know our own motivation and intent. As long as even a small part of us still wants to destroy, because of grief, need, rage or whatever, then we are still in patriarchal bondage (negative karma), and will not be able to work effectively as healers, mediums and so on, because we will be giving out mixed messages, which will be received in the psyche of those whom we think we are helping. Moreover it is important for our safety as women moving in patriarchy that we possess a clarity of intent.

Clarity comes about with the recognition that the things that happen to us are the direct results of our thoughts and visualisations (negative or positive). Clarity depends upon the ability to trace these linkages from one's mind to the results of its activity.

Thus by eradicating all harmfulness from our intent, we can neither be harmed. It is that simple and that precise.

This is not to say however that we cannot still become enraged. Righteous rage is the force of feeling that comes from our perception of our oppression and the state of the planet today. But this type of rage is a motive force for change. It doesn't gnaw away at our fabric in the same way as do the emotions arising from our self/other destruct programmes. Having once named the source of our pain, through the awareness that Raja Yoga can open up for us, we are then able to proceed away from self-obsession, to do the urgent work of healing and restoring the balance to Earth and her inhabitants as our calling directs us.

Connecting heaven and earth through Aum - the sacred sound.

"In the beginning was the Word and the Word was with God and the Word was God." *The Gospel according to St John.*

In the ancient Indian scriptures we read repeatedly of Aum or Om, the sacred word. God is nameless, formless, but when God projects or manifests into creation, light and sound emerge as God's primary attributes. Aum is the primordial sound that links spirit to matter, the audibility of the life stream. Aum is the supreme mantra - representing the cycle of creation, preservation, destruction and silence. Aum is the universal vibration that underlies everything in the universe. When we chant this holy sound, we connect ourselves to the infinite, and place ourselves beyond thought, and into rhythm with the infinite, divine, eternal cycle.

Bhakti Yoga, is the Yoga of Love. It is nothing more than the devotion of our hearts to the divine. We love the Goddess and we love the God. This is Bhakti. To love the

Mother and love the Father, and make them happy by returning their unconditional love. It is not an intellectual path and tends to involve much singing and dancing, music and celebration. But despite the child-like qualities of its practice it is also taught as a path to enlightenment. Although God is originally seen as separate from oneself, by chanting his or her name/s, one is eventually able to unite with the divinity. This is similar to the principles involved in Buddhist chanting, except that in Bhakti Yoga one does not say that one is invoking one's own divinity, which is of course the truth of the practice, but rather believes that by calling out and invoking the name of the divine, the deity will eventually take the devotee into its heart and they will then become enlightened.

Bhakti Yoga is best epitomised in the West by the devotees of Hare Krishna, who name Lord Krishna as their main deity. The Hare Krishna devotees are practitioners of Bhakti Yoga, but also Raja Yoga in their moral and ethical precepts. They neither eat meat nor accept violence and there is undoubtedly a very attractive and beautiful quality about the nature of this path to God. It is also simple. Chanting the name of Krishna in all forms, since Krishna is really both male and female, over and over, will infuse the devotee with Krishna consciousness, hence saving him or her from the hell that is experienced when one becomes immersed in material life and thought.

The passivity of the men in the movement and in other devotional Yoga is very attractive. But the women too are passive, and because it is a teaching from within a patriarchal religion - Hinduism - despite the fact that it truly attempts to open the heart, women's rage is not given voice to. It is neither named nor even anticipated. A passive movement for women who have not acknowledged their anger, will not permit women to thrive spiritually. If one really looks at some of the female devotees practicing Bhakti Yoga, many of them are in one form of denial or other. Moreover male and female sexuality is not being adequately expressed within such groups, as the males may be in monk-like renunciation- or conversely there is an overemphasis on sex. This is promiscuity, not tantra (see later). However this again refers more to the human organisation that has sprung up around the worship of the deity.

Nevertheless the truth of these devotional teachings is undeniable. That heart-centred being is the only possibility, if we are to live lives of joy and growth. No other way of seeing the world, other than perceiving from our hearts is safe. Lovingly chanting the names of our beloveds, be they divine or human (even the Gods are only spiritual energies that we perceive, the names for which have been created by our human minds) infuses us with love consciousness and is a protection against the negative effects of the wanderings of our minds. Where thought and energy flow, attention goes (this is one of the basic principles of Hawaiian shamanism - Kahuna). So we cannot afford to be too careful when attempting to protect ourselves. This repetition of God's name is known as Japa. The problem with many common forms of Bhakti Yoga that I know of, is that they invoke the male names of God. God in male form is the assumption.

We need to consider redressing the balance by calling on the great female Goddesses, as I have stated in the previous chapter, when talking about Tara and the Buddhist Goddesses. Indeed our self worth depends upon us calling upon our own Goddess natures. We can invoke the powers of Kali and Shakti. We could look amongst the ranks of the great and little known Goddesses to furnish us with information about how to regain our power and wholeness. By invoking divine female beings, we summon their qualities into our own lives, as we become one with them. Or we could choose names for ourselves and our lovers to symbolise our divine qualities, and then practice Japa - calling them forth.

Naming is terrifically powerful and it is why a change of name is often important to accompany a change of life state, to match the person in their higher self form. This is why most spiritual aspirants are given new names by their Gurus. Feminists know however that the true Guru is within, it is the teacher of the higher self, and a new name may come whilst in a state of vision or meditation, that describes our highest being. These names are all good to repeat. In fact there is power to be gained in repeating any name that inspires us to love. Become the lover. **LOVE. LOVE. LOVE.**

Karma Yoga is the Yoga of virtuous action in the business of daily living. Mothers are natural Karma Yogins. They do not need to go and live in an ashram, (the spiritual household of a guru) to perform selfless service without thought of gain or reward. Children are the perfect Gurus.

The problem here is that society sanctions the rejection of this powerful female experience. To serve one's family and children is considered a choice of equal weighting with going out to work for a living. In reality many women do not feel they make a conscious choice anyway, so great are the economic and emotional pressures against serving selflessly. Looking after one's family is considered so demeaning anyway, although conservative moralists, who see it as a burden, try to impose it on women. However their view is that society needs women to do it for the sake of family values. On a spiritual level, serving one's or someone else's family is nevertheless practicing Karma Yoga and confers great spiritual benefits. However everything about the patriarchal economic system is set up to support those who work for profit, either for themselves or others, with less importance put upon working for the welfare of others.

Consequently, women are discouraged from the work of nurturing their families, which is nevertheless at least a part of their natures, as the natural mothers and healers on the planet. Yet even when they do go out into the work economy they tend to fall into the areas of service. However, serving people without really wanting to is not Karma Yoga. You have to really want to do Karma Yoga.

As we become more healed, by the process of understanding and controlling ourselves more, so we progress and become more the healer and less the needer. Holy women are healer women. Healing is Karma Yoga, because it comes from an intention to serve the Earth and her peoples and her creatures. However, because of the patriarchal emphasis, woman's natural healing quality becomes warped. Too many women are serving in suffering with a negative attitude.

We need to honour our children and those we care for, and to know that this work we do is the most sacred work of all, in spite of its restricted value in the narrow, yet overemphasised field of the patriarchal marketplace. We should only do work that we enjoy. If we don't enjoy our work then we can either change the work or our attitude, whichever is the easier. Despite the difficulties, once we have found our life-work, we will become truly inspired. In the meantime, please be assured that all work is virtuous, when it is done in a spirit of love and acceptance. Becoming a feminist is selfless work, and it is the service that the planet requires of you right now!

Women of integrity and discipline need to follow the fastest route to ego-free bliss (complete de-programming from patriarchal dictates). One way of knowledge is through **Jnana Yoga**. Jnana Yoga is also known as the Yoga of Knowledge, or Right discrimination. Jnana Yogis can pierce through the veil of illusion to perceive the truth in all things directly. They have penetrating insight. An adherent of this path challenges themselves to be like the fellow known as the "Superior Man" in the I Ching, the ancient Chinese philosophy of the law of change, which offers guidelines for correct behaviour. The practitioner of Jnana Yoga must strengthen themselves in every way, by willingly and consciously eliminating everything in themselves which is inferior, dishonest or ignorant. In other words, consciously eliminating one's karma. This person is sworn to continual self-improvement, and they can know the truth because of their direct connection to the divine. It could also be called all that encompasses being "impeccable", in the sense of what Carlos Castaneda's teacher, Don Juan, calls an "impeccable warrior". A Jnana Yoga practitioner is a warrior of the spirit, who possesses inner resolve, and is above all true to herself. It demands the pursuit of mental clarity in all things, and the willingness to become different from others, in that whilst the majority of humanity is in a state of slumber, the Jnana Yogi is awake and determined to remain so.

The practice consists of intense and thoughtful contemplation of one's life experience, in order to distinguish the true from the false at every step. It demands the overcoming of all duality, and the ability to enter into one's true centre, away from the extreme states into which most people drift, out of their control. Once you have mastered Jnana Yoga, you are, in the words of Castaneda's Yaqui Indian sorcerer teacher, no longer like a leaf at the mercy of the wind. You have cultivated extreme control over your emotional body, you have found stability and steadfastness. Jnana Yoga is the commitment to the acquisition of wisdom, to Sage consciousness, and requires the gathering and harnessing of that part of oneself known as **"the will"**. Buddhist insight meditation also develops Jnana qualities. Clarity is insight.

Many of us feminists have incredible integrity and a passionate commitment to life, as well as to ourselves and each other. We are naturals as Jnana Yogis. We cannot tolerate spiritual wrongness, particularly in ourselves, and we are committed to seeking the truth of every situation, even if it means we have been wrong, even up to the minute of realisation. We possess the humility and compassion to accept responsibility for our actions. This is because we have intense spiritual longing, and so we are prepared to lay our cards on the table and even go through the painful - at the time - process of having our ego bubble burst, for the sake of growth and knowledge. This is easier to say than to experience, but it is nevertheless the fastest and most liberating way out of suffering. Jnana Yoga leads to deliverance.

However it is not an easy path to follow unless one is fortunate enough to meet a spiritual teacher and Jnana Yogi who is herself a liberated being. I did, but my programming prevented me from being grateful at the time, although of course the emergence of my blocks was part of the teaching. My first teacher was a wise-woman, warrior, sorcerer, feminist yogi, healer/witch who instilled into me a right consciousness, often at cost to her own health, so great was my resistance. Nevertheless, she managed, against many odds, to transmit her wisdom to me, for which I am truly grateful.

I am attempting to show how the different yoga paths, either in combination of several or all of them, can offer a non-patriarchal way for women to step out of the hopelessness that an empty spiritual life pre-empts. This is the spiritual life that I am attempting to define, live and pass on to women who are open and ready. It is by no means the only way to feminist empowerment, but it is my own particular route. As I said, I would not presume to suggest that a spiritual discipline (in the non moralistic sense of the word) is necessary for all feminists and I would welcome the day when such practice is no longer necessary, although I personally enjoy my spiritual life, which has now become my whole life. But there are many people who have less karma than myself to deal with, and they will no doubt have their own unique teachings to transmit. May they be blessed in their quest to bring happiness to people.

My own task is to offer encouragement and knowledge

to those women who feel attracted to the way of the **Dharma** (acting in accordance with the Divine law) through Hindu or Buddhist paths of wisdom, but who may have found these traditions to be deeply embedded with unacceptable sexism. They may have been quite put off by all the emphasis on masters and gurus that these traditions encompass. My purpose is to uncover the universal truth at the centre of these teachings, and to present it in non-sexist form. Because the fact is that many of the yogic teachings do offer us certain wise methods and unshakeable spiritual truths that can help us not only to get our act together, but more importantly to keep it together. Other spiritual and magical or mystical teachings can offer the same truth, because the truth is universal, but they dress it in a different language and place it within different cultural contexts. I am attempting to show how there can be liberation from suffering for both men and women by practicing these bodies of knowledge.

The feminist truth implicit in yoga is that it offers us a technology of ecstasy, which is a tremendously healing force both to ourselves and those around us. Ecstasy is a "new" frequency, in the sense that more and more people will be tuning into this level of being than ever before. Natural ecstasy is the natural drug that we are being led to as the healing of the 20th century progresses to embrace all of humanity.

Ecstasy is the frequency that heals us and the earth.

Ecstasy is most definitely a feminist frequency, it is the prerogative of all women and all people that has been stolen from us in our surrender to the patriarchal view of life. We are all tuned to the patriarchal frequency of fear, chaos, and hostility. No one asks us if we agree. We are given no choice. But there is a choice. We can spend more and more time in ecstasy and less and less in suffering, because as we suffer, so we preclude ourselves from becoming ecstatic. Ecstasy is a tremendous energy, which when exhibited by female shamans and witches, mediums and other women who link directly to the source of consciousness, has been the cause of fear by patriarchal emissaries. Patriarchy contains within it a massive plot to stamp out ecstasy, but we must reclaim this force without fear. Yoga gives us some tools to do this. Therefore it is, at its truth, a feminist ally. Moreover it creates great health benefits. I encourage all women to practice yoga, but to be aware not to fall into the patriarchal limitations that surround some schools of thought within yoga. In order to stay free of this, once she has studied and is able to monitor the effects of her practice she should define her own yoga, perhaps under sincere guidance at first, which will allow her to liberate herself as soon as possible.

One of the most modern channellings of a type of yoga, **Kundalini Yoga**, comes to us from the Sikh teacher, formerly of India and latterly of USA, Yogi Bhajan. He has done a lot of teaching for women to help increase grace, strength and stamina. Although he is not a woman, he has tremendous respect and moreover true seeing of the power of women, as creatresses from whom all human life comes. He recognises that the liberation of women is the key to happiness on Earth, and that the patriarchal bounds under which we labour are the cause of all suffering. Sikhism is the youngest of the world religions, tracing its origins from Guru Nanak, who declared the way to God, or **at-one-ment**, through the power of Shabd, or the inner music of the sacred sound. The simplicity and wisdom of Sikh teachings is in alignment with the ecological consciousness that is necessary to regenerate our own mum - the Earth. Therefore many of the women who emerge from this training of Kundalini Yoga are formidable spiritual teachers in their own right, possessing the power of selfhood and conscious of the need to liberate their sisters both within and outside of Sikhism (the word Sikh means simply truth seeker). In addition to this, the priority on right relationships between men and women is important for restoring the balance between the male and female energies on the planet. Yogi Bhajan teaches a dynamic form of Yoga/meditation known as White Tantra, where partners learn to connect male and female polarities through the heart chakra and all the chakras, thereby truly fusing in love with the divine. It follows that women who actualise this knowledge have learnt how to love their partners, their children and the earth they walk on. Much time is spent in exercises to encourage higher states of consciousness, learning how to get high from within ourselves. Therefore the teachings of the 3HO (Happy, Healthy, Holy Organisation) are particularly appropriate to women who are or have been hooked on external stimuli-compulsive behaviour patterns of pain dulling, like drugs, food or excessive alcohol intake. By learning how to get high naturally, we can overcome our cravings and at the same time develop our strength and resistance to such weaknesses. Sikhs believe in God. The devotional aspects of this path of Yoga are good for women who have a lot of negative programming, in the form of over-inflated egos, which are actually due to lack of self-valuation based on neglect and not having been properly loved. In surrendering this controllingness of their natures, these women will find true humility and true devotion, which is true love, and will start to open up their views of the world.

There is also a path of Yoga known as **Tantric Yoga**. Tantric Yoga sets out to overcome the duality between person and God, that we are unable to bridge without spiritual practice, through realisation of the union between Shiva (the Tantric personification of the Supreme Deity) and Shakti, his consort as cosmic power, or force. This relationship is symbolised by male and female energies, hence Tantric practices are designed to fuse these two polarised energies. The purpose of Tantra is to achieve as rapid as possible liberation from the cycles of birth and death, as is the purpose of most Yoga teachings. However Indian Tantra raises the Kundalini energy to do this, because when the force is raised up the spine to the top of the head, one's vision becomes enlightened, thus illusory dualistic perception is dissolved. It is basically a way of freeing oneself from the limitations of mind and senses, and involves charging oneself up with earth force, or pranic energy. In other words, getting "turned on" in order to expand awareness. It involves learning how to feel with the chakra body, rather than the physical body. The chakras are sacred psychic sites on the body, where energy accumulates. It depends not, as so many yoga teachings within the ancient tradition do, on transcending the senses, but rather on immersing oneself totally into the senses. Refusal to honour the body the creator and creatress have given us is, as I said earlier, sacrilege. Our bodies are capable of experiencing exquisite pleasure, and it is errant and male-centred of us to think that the pleasures of our bodies are only there for us to overcome and thus prove our ability to triumph over the baseness of nature. But then, woman-hating is all about trying to show the baseness of nature and the superiority of culture, and look where that has got us!

Modern day Tantrists immerse themselves in all aspects of life. Instead of going around obstacles, or shunning them, Tantrists immerse themselves in the centre of their resistance, in order to gain their liberation from releasing their attachments. They even welcome the painful lessons in their lives as a way to speed them to self-realisation, as they humbly open themselves and accept the lessons that they realise they have attracted, in order to help them to the quickest possible freedom. They are rapid changers of karma. Tantra is the art of awareness in all things, and the opening of consciousness to a wider sphere. Therefore they believe in and practice experiencing the fullness of sensations that life brings them.

As they do not shun pain, if it is appropriate to their growth, and the former may be the condition they experience more of at first, they also cultivate awareness of the exquisite pleasure that we are capable of, as a means of healing, both oneself and others. Tantric Yoga involves practices and meditations where mutually consenting adults may do anything that raises the force, or Kundalini power. They believe in breaking down human imposed limitations that block off awareness and ecstasy.

Sexual synchronicity (Tantric sex) is an important part of the Tantric practice, where this type of "magic" is applicable. Sexual intercourse is often the basis of meditation, but Tantra is not only sexual, and is often misunderstood, by minds that turn to jelly at the mere suggestion of non-patriarchal, non-reproductive orientated sexuality. Tantra is in fact vibrational synchronicity between people, and between people and their environment, which leads to ecstasy. Whilst sexual intercourse is obviously a good way to access this, as the fusion between male and female energies is a deeply divine and empowering force, it is by no means the only way as the work of Yogi Bhajan shows us.

Tantric Yoga unsurprisingly fell into disrepute in the East under European, Victorian invasion. But it was a woman loving path. The divine was worshipped as the Supreme Mother and as Shakti, the universal creative energy, and the Tantric was not, as in many other types of Yoga spirituality, a devotee of any predominantly male incarnation of the divine. What was worshipped was the fusion of opposites, the entwining of Shiva and Shakti. Because of this unique emphasis, (women were equal partners with men in the pursuit of ecstasy, it is not possible to be ecstatic if you are subordinate) it could not survive under patriarchy and the censure of pleasure that was the nature of Victorian moralism. Lewd minds have corrupted any truth that remains, making Tantra synonymous with depravity, and perhaps in places where it is still formally practiced it has become as such. In fact Tantra is considered to be a path only for truly committed seekers of spirituality.

It most relates to feminists when we come to consider the nature of the feeling body, and the damage it sustains under patriarchal ideas about love and sexuality. The constant negation of ourselves throughout life, as we deny our bodies, our lustiness in our own sexuality and our wild natures, takes a terrible toll on us in the sense that we learn early on how to cut off from feeling, physical and emotional, if we are going to survive.

"Nice girls don't". "She got what she asked for"... and all the other confusing things we pick up about our sexuality makes us close up, if we are to protect ourselves from rape, unwanted male attention and damaging relationships. So we become asexual as our protection. But this also damages us, because expression of our sexuality is a key to our tuning in to the frequency of ecstasy ,and the power of the life force, with or without a male partner. If we dare not express this aspect of our creativity, we are truly being repressed and robbed of our joy. We need to become fully tantric in order to heal ourselves from our habit of dullness. As we wait switched-off, for Mr Right to come and turn us on, we stay sad and angry at what we have allowed to happen to us. But we may wait in vain, because it is our job to become tantric even without, or before him, and then to teach him some of our magic.

We must become tantric in order to heal ourselves, each other and above all the Earth, who needs us to give her some of the energy we conjure. Because Tantra is white magic. It is good healing magic. As we pulsate with the energy we gain from tantric fusion, some of it pours back into the Earth as we infuse her with healing and love.

The main thing is that we heal the Earth, firstly by healing ourselves and each other - bodies, psyches, spirits, souls. We must connect to the Goddess within ourselves as well as the God. Both male and female in perfect fusion are necessary to create new healthy life. But by becoming woman-centred in our quest for spiritual knowledge and healing, we will redress the balance that has gone wrong from over-worshipping the male side of the divine partnership. But we should not only worship the Goddess in our misguided anger towards men, when the truth is uncovered, because men need our love and our compassion too, so that they can reveal their Godlike qualities. In a sense we are the leaders in the matter of consciousness. By loving and extending our true passion to men, who are also the victims of patriarchal mind twisting, we will encourage them to show their true strength, as opposed to their macho strength, which is destroying our planet. By becoming woman-centred, we will create the conditions in which to love and serve our sisters. Only then will we be able to pass on to men our powerful message of love and hence our true feminist teachings. We are amongst those women who have been directed to find and lead the way now!

I think that we can find our initial way through religion, whilst adhering to the matristic roots of the traditions I have been describing.

Eventually however, there may come a time when we need to create and develop our own unique religious practice based on our experience and the effects of the teachings we have been following. In other words until we are sure of our humility and correctness, it may be wise to follow a pre-defined pattern of worship. However, once we are assured of our impeccability in all life, we can design our own model of worship, naming the components that inspire us to our divine connection. In other words we have become the priestess, not the follower. We can do this, because we know who we truly must follow and therefore can do no wrong.

Our lives will become our religion, our religion will be our life. There can be no separation at this level.

Let us find the inspiration for our lives in the models of the Priestess/Healers of ancient pre-patriarchal cultures. Like the Chanting Priestesses of pre-Columbian Mexico, who called on the healing vibration of sound to transcend the profane. Or the pre-Aryan Yogini of the Indus valley whose supple body was a map of sacred sites.

But let's not forget that there are plenty of contemporary holy women that we must also become humble enough to see as well.

It is once again time to publicly celebrate woman. Her history, our present, and to move forwards inspired by ourselves and infused with the passion that comes from honouring ourselves as holy women.

Let us enjoy the well earned relaxation that springs from our vision of ourselves as engaged in disciplined practice of growing faith. We need to make sacred sounds, calling upon the names of the divine source of all life, to infuse our lives with its essence, to make ourselves radiant and strong. Let us pray and chant, meditate and sing and breathe deeply, pouring forth blessings upon humanity from our open hearts. Then let us rest assured that in this state, the God that we link up with in our hearts, the God that stirs up and reminds us of our purpose is the one true God. In ecstatic devotion how could we do wrong?

THE BOOK OF SIBYL

Chapter 1
Patriarchal Pattern Busting.

Feminism involves changing every cell in your body.

As we first ask for our lives to open up , and as we travel into other dimensions of reality to fuel this urge, we will find that many blocks appear to try to prevent us from stepping out of the banality of our lives that we are so drained by. We will find any reason not to go into sacred space, until the glorious time when we are so hooked by our inner lives that nothing can stop us. In other words when our true wills are engaged in our spirituality.

However it is important to be aware that these hindrances to our practice will arise, and to learn to recognise and challenge them at the outset. For example at those times when we most need to pray, we may actually find ourselves resisting, disguised in such reasonable sounding excuses as the needs of the children, work, the house, the shopping or whatever. But this is just part of our negative karma at work- our devilish shadows, that use tricks to stop us from going into the space where we might be able to see and re-programme our weaknesses. Our resistance to entering sacred space is an aspect of our patriarchal programming.

The main thing to remember is that once you have acknowledged your need for healing, nothing must take precedence. Once you have established the firm foundation for your life, everything will quite naturally fall into place. It can indeed be painful to challenge one's own weaknesses, but let me assure you it is nothing compared to the pain of living a life of unconfronted negativity.

It is really our own unexpressed anger at ourselves and others, and our laziness which is really rooted in fear, that makes us resist jumping headlong into our inner resources. But what have we really got to lose, compared to what we are bound to gain?

This is why in some ways, committing oneself to the discipline of a practice, like chanting Nam-Myoho-Renge-Kyo or Kundalini Yoga, is a way of ensuring peace of mind. Becoming a Buddhist or a Yogini makes it easier for oneself. Because to be a Buddhist you have to chant and pray, that is the essential practice, and if you have to chant then you are indeed fortunate, because it is in chanting that one remembers what are life's priorities. Just as in the same way if you commit yourself to a way of life like Kundalini Yoga, you know that the basis of that practice is to carry out morning Sadhana (spiritual discipline), which is the very foundation of your spiritual life.

Clearly, the only existing religions which hold validity for women today, are those which offer us tools for self-empowerment. By putting our faith firmly in our own hands, we can increase our well-being and life energies. But if our religion does not afford us this opportunity, if it demands slavish adherence to fixed principles, if it holds no promise of joy in this life, but is merely an empty ritual to try to trick yourself and your judgemental, shaming and damning God into believing you are a decent, caring human being when you are not, then you might as well forget it. Because if your religion does not grow your religiousness, then it is massive self-deception.

Feminism involves changing every cell of your body, to root out the programming that is locked within the muscles and corpuscles. Changing the thought that causes us to suffer. Re-living the past with a consciousness of the present. Naming the pain. Erasing patriarchy from every cell.

Ecstatica

The Sacred Woman

It is tremendously healing to start seeing oneself as a sacred woman. To surround oneself with one's own holiness and the radiance that manifesting this self-belief creates. We need not wait for anyone to validate us, to say we are indeed holy, because there are probably very few people qualified to do this by virtue of their exemplicity and lovingness. There is no value in being accorded high honours by people who go home and wank over the pages of a porno magazine or agonise over cheating on their best friend. This is not to say these people are bad, just to say that they have no right to judge us. The right to lack of humility that this society allows is a slur on the character of humanity and shows the level of weakness we are collectively at today. But the problem is, when weak people are allowed to pass judgement on other people they know deep inside themselves that they should not be doing this and it makes them feel awful about themselves. Because our society does not allow us the surrender of pride, by letting us respect another person by virtue of their decency as a human being, rather than their status in the hierarchy of life, we feel bad about ourselves, because we know at a deeper level that this is not correct. Moreover we are creating karma for ourselves in not offering basic respect to another human being. We are also setting up a pattern for refusing to learn from our experience, because we deny wisdom, by denying its source.

We women are sick of not being respected by people who do not have the humility to learn from us. This has gone on for long enough and it is most definitely time for a change. Living in a world with lack of respect for other living beings is a choice to live in a fraction of the boundless possibilities. Why live a quarter life when you can live a whole one? Why settle for fear and constraint when you can have openness and laughter?

ridicule anyone talking about such experiences with any conviction, so we tend not to develop these gifts. Because that is what they are.

A woman who is a Sibyl believes in her gifts of prophecy, of divination, of mediumship. Whatever powers manifest through her are her gifts to develop and to pass on to others. Many women are currently in a state of denial regarding their not inconsiderable Sybillic tendencies. However only when she accepts and embraces these aspects of herself can she come to wholeness.

When we become Sibyls we use our telepathic sense as an equal sense with our others, rather than as unfathomable chance. We believe in our visions and dreams, and welcome them because we recognise that they contain knowledge for us that we may not have become conscious of within the bustle of our everyday activities. Sibyls act upon the information gained in their insights as if it were real, because they recognise that reality is everything they experience and they do not limit the scope of their lives according to the smallness of patriarchal predefinitions.

Sibyls are channels of knowledge from the unseen realms. The truth that utters from their mouths is the truth of past, present and future, because they travel to dimensions where there is no linear structure, and all is happening at the same time.

Unconfined by the physical body, they are able to travel astrally anywhere. They make their inner bodies strong, so that they can achieve feats of great power in the invisible worlds. Thus their subtle bodies are not weak and inactive like those of us who are hooked upon the physical world, but are able to carry out actions at the Sibyl's will.

This is the basis of the archetypal symbol of the witch on the broomstick. She is actually flying through other realms to meet the spirits that inhabit them. She is the medium engaged in receiving messages from those who are no longer in the physical world. She is the telepath who manifests at exactly the right moment she is needed.

These are the formidable, yet everyday powers of the Sibyl, who becomes our being when we are aware enough and open enough to receive her energies. We need to be like clean slates, unfilled with our own chatter in order to properly channel and manifest her presence.

However for many of us there is still work to be done, because the fact is that most of the time, the majority of women experience a continual and repetitive mental dialogue, which takes a specific pattern and is triggered by certain factors. Upon meeting these factors our mental activity kicks into its conditioned response, according to our "what's in it for me" intent. We all have different scripts in which we play different roles. A lot of us think we know ourselves, but it can be an interesting, fascinating exercise to learn to spot these different selves, to name them and to come to recognise the lines that they always say.

What are the bases behind these theatrical parts that compose us? Who are these roles, and when we have discovered who they all are and what triggers them into action, who will be left? Most of these parts that we unwittingly, and often unconsciously, play out in the theatre of life, demand that we be a victim of some sort. It will not do for us to be too powerful or wild. There are many weak roles available for women. Then there are the supposedly strong roles, for the ball-breakers, because they are the control merchants who must always come out on top. These are the ones that have the secret sexual fantasies like being tied up and chastised, because really inside of themselves they know they have no humility to anyone and they know that in order to find ecstasy they will have to surrender their control. All in all, there are a lot of angry roles available to women, especially a lot of seething lines. "I'll get even", is one that is often

Sacred women are not suffering women. They are ecstatic women. They bathe in consciousness as they open their hearts and souls to its torrent. They do not fear, because it is in fear that we close down and lose our awareness. Thus we can become sick and die.

It is absolutely essential that we realise that the sacred is everywhere and that we start to believe this in our daily lives. There is no separation between us and God. God is in everything. However, the important thing is to remember this, when getting bogged down in the minutiae of daily life. As soon as our thoughts come in and we let our attachment to them control us, we tend to lose our awareness of the sacred as we fall into patterns of negativity.

God has not deserted us, hard as this may be to believe sometimes, but we have temporarily snapped our connection. In allowing our calm to dissipate, we forget our love, and the task is for us to remember, and remember and remember it, over and over again, until we no longer have this separation in our lives. This is why we do need to make time for sacred work. In fact it is absolutely crucial that we make time for our religious practice, whatever that may be, so that as each day dawns we strengthen our faith.

Gradually, it will happen that we gain in strength and clarity through our meditation and devotional practices and our commitment to self-knowledge. So we will naturally become more receptive to subtler energies in the universe. Yogis talk of the Siddhis, which are the powers that develop alongside assiduous practice of Yoga, and include the development of such senses as clairvoyance, levitation and telepathy. There will be an increase in our use of so called paranormal senses, although of course this terminology reflects the sense of spiritual limitation humanity feels at this time.

Psychic powers are perfectly normal, as are psychic experiences. However there is a tendency to undermine and encountered.

The main thing to know is that all these fragmented little people inside our heads that go to make us up, are there from a very young age, they never say anything new, they always stick within the limited confines of their behaviour patterns, and all we have to do is to first witness them and then name them for the little devils to lose all their power.

To know herself is one of the hardest things for a woman to do and one of the most pressing. This is because it's a question of weeding out all the little splits inside one, that arise from time to time in certain situations. One will have to become conscious of one's mind workings, so that energy is not lost in draining oneself with one's pre-patterned thought processes. You might be surprised at how much your view of yourself depends upon the nature of these tiny mind habits. They can mean the difference between liking ourselves or not, the difference between our being weak or strong.

The point is that there is nothing to feel guilty or hopeless about. Realise that, to some extent, your mind is not your own. You have been programmed to judge other women, to want to bring about another woman's downfall, just as you have been programmed to see every man as a potential mate. Where "me first" is the guiding principle, how could it be otherwise? Only if we start to put others before ourselves can we become free of this pattern. But to do this we will need to be healed enough from our own needs and past unlovedness.

Patriarchy depends for its continuance upon the type of downfall plotting that ceaselessly goes on in the average mind of a woman in 20th century life. It depends upon your mind-blocked judgement and feeling of separation from every other living being, because it needs you to compete, in order to stoke it up. Your competitiveness and your negativity are patriarchy's fuel. This is why looking at life, without intent to classify or judge, needs to be aimed for. This is meditation. Meditation is not a question of sitting with the eyes closed on a cushion, trying to shut up one's mind, although this is good practice, if one can do it. What meditation actually is, is the pure observation of life as it passes by the window of one's consciousness. Meditation is a way of living. It is life with one's awareness kicked into action.

The best place to start looking with aware eyes is within oneself. It is here, deep inside the myriad, mucky waters of one's own being, that one can discover a fascinating world of faulty programming. Programming that actually gets us into all sorts of trouble and doesn't further us in any way. Programming that leaves us thinking "oh, I wish I hadn't done/said that."

We should not be angry with ourselves when we find out how compulsively mind-set we are, how repetitively, uncontrollably destructive we can be. Instead, we should just take the time to retreat, to face up to our our worst selves with compassion and acceptance and to resolve not to be beaten by patriarchy, as so many women before us have been. We should be prepared to drop out of situations that drain us and in which we are prompted to behave badly. Although even if we do react negatively, as long as we practice awareness of ourselves as we do so, we will come face to face with ourselves which is no bad thing. Practice makes perfect. Nothing is more pressing than to learn about ourselves in order to heal ourselves. If this takes the shape of numerous confrontations with one's shadows then so be it. For it is in truly facing ourselves and being able to face who we are, without the frills of patriarchal lying to ourselves to make ourselves feel O.K, that we will gain most healing and freedom to become who we truly are.

Ecstatica

The Nature of Patriarchal Dialogue

There are different types of internal mental struggle that women under patriarchy experience. It depends upon the view of the self and the world around them that the person grew up with. Sometimes the dialogue is deeply buried within the soul and the psyche and can be difficult to detect by others. These women are very good at covering up their pain. They cover it up from themselves best of all. These are women who are in denial. They are in denial of their own pain, of other women's pain, of the Earth's pain. They believe everything is fine, even though they aren't happy. But they aren't really aware that they aren't happy, and this makes liberation very difficult for these women, because they do not think they need to become liberated. Or worse, they think that they already are.

Other women have a nearer-the-surface type dialogue, that can more easily be seen and read by others. This type of energy under the confines of patriarchal mind space is more outwardly focused.

Their intent is easier to read and therefore one can see and know what they are thinking. In a way these women with nearer the surface internal dialogues are less damaged at their core and can therefore become more easily aware of their internal processes and thus take control of them with relative ease, with the advantage that deep inside them they are relatively undamaged and quite whole. However because their suffering is not so intense, they may be less motivated to want to change their karma.

The Necessity to erase Female Negative Karma.

Patriarchy is a condition of our minds. It also constrains our minds. We must acknowledge that as women under patriarchy our thoughts are not freely our own. They are based on the competitive and combative values that define the system of greed and growth for its own sake. Everything we think is thought within a framework, and that framework is one of limitation. It is based more on what we cannot do rather than on what we can. In order to step out of these mind-bindings that are imposed on us, even from before the very first breath, as foetuses in our mothers' wombs, we need to be able to step back and take a look at what is going on deep inside each of us, and assess the validity of the "programme" for future use. This way we can reject and eject (with time and practice) what we do not consider to be constructive in our lives.

Experience, observation and of course our suffering, will eventually teach us what patterns are the most destructive to our happiness and well-being. Many of us are programmed to self-destruct the moment anything good comes into our lives. All our actions and reactions are based on fear, anger, greed etc. My own past patterns have already lost me a husband I loved, many years of my life when I could have been doing something wonderful, a couple of jobs and a couple of homes, and a million opportunities. On the other hand you could say that perhaps I had to go through all that pain to be ready to want to change it for ever. And that is what I have done, with the loving help of people who refuse to be destroyed by what they know to be not the real me, albeit a me that tries to destroy them with great force.

Nevertheless over the years, and after much desperation at their controlling me, I have come to recognise when one of those actors inside me who purport to be me, but who are not, rears their heads. I have kept a notebook and I have stalked them. I have known what is their effect on my behaviour and known that I did not feel complete whilst they were doing their work, and I have gone inside myself and challenged the little beggars. As I saw them and acknowledged that it was they, and not me, who were disrupting my happiness, they have dissipated like vapours in the sky. But it has not been easy, because some of those nasty, funny little types that live in me and off my energy, are so tricky that they will do any manner of things to be avoided, so that sometimes one cannot catch them on the first attempt. So I have learned how to be one step ahead of them by knowing their triggers and their likely fields of operation and I have set out to watch for them. Because even if I could not detect them, I knew they were going to be there. Also you can ask your friends to look out for your characters, but be aware that your characters will not like your friends on to them and they may try to destroy your friends. So they had better be very strong friends, who care about you very much, and who care very much about helping beings overcome their suffering, too much in fact to let your personalities affect them.

There are millions of different permutations of female personality that inhabit our souls at this time. The only thing to know is that all of them are completely without any compunction for our happiness as free wild spirits. They are all only there to tame us, to train and constrain us and to make sure that we do not experience the ecstasy of our connection with the divine source of life on Earth. They like to jump in most at moments when we are at our happiest. When we are feeling really good. That is when they like to attack us best. That is when we are going to be least expecting them, when we are off our guard. Then each character plays its part in blocking us, in filling us with a different set of thoughts and images, affecting us in different sites on our bodies, freezing up our energies, blocking up different chakras and disabling us from acting.

But whatever the version, it has the same purpose. To paralyse our woman energy, our joyous will to life and to turn us into stone carved women, who cannot move this way or that, who, due to their attachment to their own needs, do not care if the Earth lives or dies, who cannot move more than a few steps in either direction of life's huge circle. Whilst underneath we are in deep grief, in seething anger at ourselves and each other because we hate how we are. We feel we have missed the boat to happiness.

All of these negative activities are our karma. Karma is the cause and effect of our past and present emanations in the world. It is the effect of the way we have gone about our life, as it manifests in our present situation. We both create it and suffer the effects of it. It is the results of the responses and reactions to life that we have chosen and continue to choose for ourselves and others and it stems from our view of ourselves and our environment.

Woman's negative karma is everything that is the shadow side of a woman, everything that is her darkness and that destroys happiness and well-being.

At this time in our history we are immersed in our suffering on all counts. We suffer through our parents, through our children, through our relationships with men, our bodies, and each other. We must know that when we choose to react to a situation from a victim stance, or a controller mode, this is our karma, which is both the result of our past causes and will go on to perpetuate the pattern - create more karma. Thus we live in a seemingly endless hell, because despite the moments of rapture, there is no constancy to our positivity and hence no growth.

I am here to tell you that this is not the way it need be. My mission here is to wake you up. How many of us can say that we are truly happy with our lives? That we wake each day infused with energy at the thought of doing our life's work? How many of us can say that we feel as though we are in control of our own lives and that we are practicing free will in our lives?

If we cannot say that this is the case, if we are not happy

- if we are living out a life to someone else's dictates - if our life is not the one we would choose - then we have no right to flinch and shy away from the knowledge that is being offered to us here. Because unless we are a part of the solution to the world's problems, then we must be a part of the problem. It's time we stood up to take responsibility for the miserable quality of life we are bringing to this planet.

I know it sounds harsh. But you are not being chastised, and there is help at every corner for those who will be brave enough to wake themselves up from their slumberous fog and start to live with purpose and balance. It is never, ever too late.

It is absolutely crucial to our happiness that we erase our negative karma as women, and create lives based on love, truth and respect.

We have tremendous force and female power tied up in our negative energy - the force of our unleashed destruction is phenomenal - so that if we could turn this power about into a positive, creative one, its healing value would be tremendous. So it is important not only for ourselves, but for all the world, for all other living beings, that we start to change our suffering into joy. We cannot continue to live in such pain, the pain of unchanged karma.

Please know that it is quite possible to change. To break the patterns for ever, to go pattern busting. So that neither you, nor anyone around you, need live in pain ever again. All it takes is practice and determination. And above all faith in yourself and the belief that you are really a beautiful, lovely being in your essence. At your core. Creating the space, the vacuum, where once these pre-programmed patterns inhabited, will leave a whole life to discover, to re-cover and to choose who and what you are going to be. Into that space can flood a whole new range of experience as endless as life itself. You will be able to wake each day and approach life

234

with the fluidity of water, as it takes you along on the fast flowing current - The Way of the Tao.

Once you begin to sincerely want to break the patterns of the lifetimes of suffering behaviour that you are used to, all manner of challenges and crises are going to arise, to try to throw you off course, to challenge your endurance and faith. The only thing that really matters in changing our negative karma is that we keep on trying. We may die still trying to change, but it doesn't matter. There must be no attachment to perfection. There can be no such thing. All that matters is the sincerity of your desire, because it is here where your peace and joyfulness lay waiting in readiness for you. Learn to laugh at yourself. It isn't that important. All that matters is that you clean your slate like a blackboard as you go along each day.

The Nature of Karma

The nature of karma is such that when it surfaces it can make a woman completely forget her originality. It ascends from our depths like a dark cloud, extinguishing the burning spark of creativity, making us forget who and what we are. Leaving us alive, but only just, like an amorphous bundle of indiscriminateness, unable to complete or carry out any acts of decency and power. This forgetting who one is, is a common occurrence in the early days of un-covering your glorious selfhood. In fact it is likely to happen so frequently in the beginning, that one can despair. The times of purpose and passion may indeed be less than the times of depressed nothingness, but do not give up. These are the seeds and they will surely grow.

The tendency at the beginnings of the journey to self-discovery is to feel overwhelmed at the depth of embeddedness of one's karmic life patterns. Disturbed nights, bad dreams, self-loathing are all likely tendencies. Perhaps you just want to hide away because you are so uncertain of your reactions and so out of control of them. Realise that this is actually a positive stage in your life and a period of great growth and acceleration, because it means you are getting serious about your life and not willing to go around damaging people. It means that you are actually starting to take responsibility for yourself and your effect on the world around you. This represents true spiritual progress.

It may be that at this time in your healing you need to take the time to go inside yourself and to come to terms with your life to date. Many women are horrified once they become aware of themselves. Once outwardly confident, successful women can be reduced to wrecks of distraught, hopelessness once they realise the power of their negative effect. Once they could destroy all in their path and walk on by, because they did not take responsibility for their acts and thoughts. But a little knowledge is a temporarily painful thing. To admit to oneself of one's own karma can leave one feeling bereft and unable to function in the world one previously breezed through without a care. These are the times when we must strengthen our faith and turn to prayer and chanting, yoga or other technologies of happiness to see us through.

We may feel like this is the correct time to go into healing sanctuary or retreat, and we should make it a priority to organise our lives to do so. Indeed this is the true meaning of retreat - a period of tranquillity in which to rest and regenerate one's energies whilst coming to terms with the seeding of one's new being. Retreat is not a matter of doing nothing and just crashing out and escaping life. Retreat is a planned withdrawal from normal life, within which one is fully aware. It may be that as one's self-knowledge grows, and more and more awareness of our patterns emerges, the retreat may have to be very long indeed. In which case we should think of ourselves as caterpillars in cocoons, who one day are without doubt going to emerge as beautiful butterflies.

The Practice of Self-Stalking

One of the most important psychic skills a woman can learn to use is the practice of self-awareness or self-stalking. Self-stalking is like running a magnetic tape in one's own body which picks up vibrations and emanations and relates them back to the conscious mind. In other words, a systems check.

At first it is important to do this every morning, in order to take control of the direction of one's life as it is lived on a daily basis. Even a short time of self-stalking can completely change one's assemblage point - the place where one is coming from emotionally and energetically - re-orientating the person towards a positive direction.

For a few moments she needs to listen to her own inner state of being and decide if it is a constructive mode in which to operate. More often than not, it will not be and the chance to change it comes, often just in letting go completely, in lying on the ground, simply "stopping", interrupting the flow of wrong direction thoughts and energies that are taking you to stress and pressure, dumping thoughts and struggles, emptying the mind.

A common response from women when offered this opportunity to change their lives is - "I don't have time for this". But when you think how much time you might otherwise waste engaged in unproductive struggle and anger, how can you afford not to practice this short daily exercise?

Chapter 2
The Breath is the Key to Life.

As soon as you start to think, you stop breathing properly. If, on the other hand, you are concentrating on your breathing you will not get lost in a pattern of thinking. The internal dialogue that fills in our mind space, like a never ending record stuck on a groove, can be ceased by deep, powerful breathing. If we remember to breathe, we will forget to think. And if we forget to think we will no longer limit and define ourselves according to the narrowest restrictions that are self-imposed in order not to disrupt the safe, old order. As we breathe we infuse our lives with energy and we let go of old, stuck patterns that have carved us in stone for aeons. We breathe deep into our bellies, our centres of womanhood and feel the power grow. As we breathe peacefully, the batteries charge. Air - good, fresh, clean air is the fuel of our bodies. Even more than food do we need oxygen. We must get this air as a basic human need.

Many of us do not fully realise this and it is a reason why women living permanently in cities cannot really relax and find enough space to be creative. Many of us have lost our way completely and are stumbling around the cities as bag-ladies and mad women who have become stuck in a mind-warp. Because we cannot get access to air in the cities, we cannot find the key to change the pattern, and we are doomed to tread the wheel as it ceaselessly turns, until such a day as the spirit can find a way to intervene to change our circumstances for us.

This is why breath is a feminist issue and why women should feel so rightly angry at the stealing of our oxygen. Our life-force is being cut off, as we and our children, the

Earth and all her creatures struggle to breathe. Patriarchy is intent on suffocating us.

Thus it is not surprising that as we choke on the thinness and weakness of the ozone damaged air around us, we become more and more crazed, turning to ever more destructive patterns. Only Yoga and proper breathing can start to liberate us from the shackles of our destructive mind conditioning.

Using the breath to still the mind and heal oneself

By sitting quietly and watching the rhythm of our uncontrolled breath, we can begin to gain some insight into our patterns. As we think, so we breathe. It is a very healing exercise to grab some control over our lives, by practicing watching our own breathing. Only when we have become fully conscious of our breath, when we have unbroken awareness of the rhythm of inhalation and exhalation of our bodies, have we tuned into a frequency from which we might know divine consciousness.

Practicing silent meditation on the emptiness of the mind, through cultivating awareness of the breath, is a very good, safe way to begin one's meditative practice. Because if we stop giving off destructive emanations, then we will stop attracting these energies from others. Breath awareness takes us to the core of ourselves, the neutral, central place from which we can witness external social life rather than participate in it. This small retreat offers us a pause, in which to re-orientate ourselves, to change the balance, so that we can start to attract good, healthy, positive factors. We are gaining that little bit more control over our lives as the patterns of them become clear.

This method of meditation is so simple and safe. It can be done without any expense, one's breath is free. All you need is a quiet space, a cushion, and perhaps some natural scented incense, flowers and candles to create a little temple within your room.

In this practice you are worshipping nobody. But as you concentrate upon your own rhythms you naturally feel more peace and harmonious energy, so your own power will grow.

When you first read about this, or start practicing this technique, you might think "oh,how boring". But the depth of the practice goes beyond words. As you focus, you can just go more and more into your breath, to the point that boredom no longer exists, because you have gone beyond the bounds of such a concept. This is the true possibility of breath meditation, but you will need to be patient with your-self and to just keep coming back without judgement to the central focus of the exercise, which is your breath.

Become aware, while watching your breath, whether it is comfortable or not. Are the inhale and exhale matched? Are you having to strive and struggle to breathe? Gradually adjust your breath rhythm so that it feels comfortable, and maintain your awareness for as long as you can. When thoughts come in, do not attach to them, let them come and go, like the waves on the sea shore. Just keep returning to your breath. As you become empty, so compassion will natu-rally arise. Emptiness is not nothingness, it is simply uncon-ditionedness. For women who fear the prospect of empti-ness, I suggest they try this practice and carry it to at least the point where they can begin to describe the qualities of medi-tation on emptiness, in glowing terms. The clarity and wis-dom that can stem from such a simple practice are unparal-leled. Also one will find that one's health naturally improves as the life state is increased. Moreover within the space that one has created, one can get the answers directly to many questions, because one comes into contact with one's own teacher within, the higher self.

As I see it, there really is no choice for the woman who is seeking freedom, but to spend as much time as possible in silencing and opening herself to her higher brain state. There is no way to gain clarity and insight but to relax deeply, whilst being wide awake. The breath techniques, or chanting Aum to a regular rhythm, can help one to enter into the space where knowledge, rather than thinking about something, is present.

Eventually there will come a time when we can see the pattern of our behaviour as it is happening, because we have become aware of what we are doing as we are doing it. We have thus arrived at the fortunate position of being able to change our karma. We have gained a moments pause in which to stop the wheel of suffering from turning for a second while we evaluate.

Seek out your sanctuary

If we contemplate our suffering with an open heart and mind, we will eventually come to see what it is caused by. At first, we will want to blame others for our pain. Our parents, our partners, our children, our employers or perhaps ourselves (falsely). Or perhaps it is the fault of the government, men, patriarchy. If we aren't happy, it is someone else's fault. This is the commonest pattern of response. If something goes wrong for us, it must be somebody else's fault.

This is only one way of looking at life. Alternatively, we could turn it about and see that every cause for pain contains its own lesson. That each new suffering drives us further towards seeking liberation from the cycle. We could bless each hardship as an opportunity.

The fact is that men are not the cause of our pain, nor are governments or nations. What really causes us to suffer are our attachments - to our own thoughts, to our own desires, to our pain and to our needs. The thinking mind is the cause of all women's suffering. For example, we look totally outside of ourselves for our fulfilment - to men, to possessions, to children, to work, to holidays,to food, to things. We attach to things that are going to make us feel better, without realising that once the thing has passed we will then feel worse. There is no constancy in this external sense attachment, and it can only be the cause of perpetuating our suffering. Happiness that does not well up from deep inside ourselves, but that depends upon an external trigger is not true happiness and will be succeeded by great pain. This is the natural law, and no one can change it.

But there is one way to change this law, and that is to go inside one's own being to find happiness, where it is constant and there is no dependency upon anyone or anything else. This is the true purpose of meditation. To grow our own happiness from inside ourselves, so that we can never be the victims of disappointment again. It just depends on how much we want to break out. On whether we have reached the point where we are no longer prepared to live in pain and suffering.

The fact is that any woman can break out of patriarchy if she sincerely wants to and she can do so by cultivating stillness and returning to the neutral point of her mind, from where she gives out nothing negative. This is her sanctuary. Her safe place within herself. This is the room of her own that can be as big and as empty as she wants. Or she can furnish it with her imagination and her love. The choice is hers.

From the safety of this room she can learn to watch and to witness. To observe herself so that she may come to know herself and see how she is programmed for her own or others' pain. This is the true practice of retreat - a planned withdrawal from the activities of the mind and the senses. It has to be this way, because the mind and the senses are set on self/other destruct.

Everything which comes into being must also pass away. This is the nature of existence. It is the simple truth of life, as observed by the Buddha. Nothing is forever. Things come and they go away again. Happiness, ecstasy, joy, rapture, where they are gained from outside causes, are merely fleeting moments, to be replaced by the depths of despair and sadness. By attaching to such things when they come, we are bound to suffer when they go.

The only thing that we can depend upon is ourselves. Our own unconditioned mind. It just is. That's its beauty. Only this realisation can provide us with the simple source of joy and happiness.

We need to seek space more and more and to take refuge in the sanctuary of our unconditioned minds. To take refuge from the inconsistency and hence unsafety of the world of mind that we call "reality". Within that safe sanctuary we will discover another reality which is more real, because it is natural, neutral and unconditioned. It just is. The peace of having no agenda is undescribable. This is why we need to meditate. Just to learn how to be. Like plants and trees, we simply are and we endure. Without judgement, without blame, we remain rooted to the earth and observe from the huge golden chamber of our minds as life passes the window of our consciousness, like a movie. This is the place from where our wisdom stems. It can take time, perseverance, effort and practice, but when we eventually break through, we reach the other side of suffering. Eventually we will reach heaven, here on earth.

Breaking through our resistance can be easier, if we remind ourselves that conditioned reality is patriarchy. Life in patriarchy is not fun. True there are some high moments. But they pass, leaving us bereft and seeking, like drug addicts, the next high experience, desperately seeking stimuli, because we cannot bear to face the pain of our lives, and we have not been trained to see emptiness as a pleasant experience. This is the true nature and dead-endedness of conditioned reality. But it depends upon whether or not we have a vested interest in remaining within the patriarchal set of values. Many of us do, and it is time to be honest with ourselves and acknowledge that we are more attached to these values than we would give ourselves credit for. In meditation we will be able to go to awareness of this truth about ourselves, and to see what are the patriarchal payoffs for us, and what keeps us hooked to the wheel of karma. By connecting to our divine sacred selves, we will gain the power to overcome our fear - the fear of flying, of leaping into the abyss of faith, trust and love.

We must know that as long as we are playing the patriarchal game we are in danger. Because it is a nasty game that does not value the lives of women and children. As long as we are in competition with others to survive, as long as our success depends upon damaging others, even if we are not aware of it, we are getting nowhere in our pursuit of joy and happiness. We are stuck up a dead-end street. We are giving consensus to a reality that keeps us mean and small.

But life in unconditioned reality, undifferentiated, unclassified life, life which is just being, well that is a different matter entirely. As we sit in our truly safe and protected space - for nothing can harm us if we have retreated from harm's way - then will we truly begin to know joy. Only it is not anything that we can name. Just pure aliveness and being. Being without agenda. That is heaven.

Eventually you will come to know the happiness of being fully in the present moment. Without need or thought of the future. The happiness of being in the present moment and not worrying about anything, because all one's life is in order. One is completely there, in one's life, innocent like a child, no longer accruing karmic debts. Each day the slate is wiped clean, but anyhow there is nothing so serious to repent of, because one's actions are naturally good, once one is aligned with the Tao.

With an expanded awareness and an ability to experience life directly as it happens, one simply is. Life is an awesome mystery, but how to live it is not. The connections between one's actions and the consequences of them become crystal clear, as we start to take full responsibility for creating our own realities. We no longer seek to blame others when things don't work out as we had hoped, but are now able to see every situation as grounds for learning and growth.

In this state of calmness and acceptance, nothing can throw us off balance as we are able to incorporate every moment of life, good and bad, into our experience and recognise that everything is both a manifestation and a part of the great spirit.

There is one thing that I forgot to mention to those of you who are thinking how lonely it must be up there in your mind-castle, divorced from the attractions of the social world. Others can join you in unconditioned reality. This is Tantra. You can be one, or you can be many, within the sacredness of that pure space. All it requires is consensus from your friends. As you meditate together, as all artificial barriers and separations between you dissolve, then, as your hearts unite, can you experience and know the bliss of true fusion.

Chapter 3
You are The Priestess of your own Temple.

Because you now have no fixed religion, but yet you are very religious, it is up to you to create your own temple. This can be a room in your home, which is used for ritual and sacred work.

The central point of your temple is the altar, which can contain any imagery that inspires you to devotional contemplation. It can be as simple as a cushion and a vase of flowers, or you can go to great lengths to build your altar, like the Hispanic healers do. You can change it as you see fit. The main thing is that it should be a space infused with your own faith, love and power, where you feel protected and can enter into communion with the divine, as it channels through your consciousness. There are some other helpful sacred tools that a woman may find helpful as an adjunct to her meditation.

1 - The Tarot

As well as meditation, a really good way to open oneself to divine energy is, naturally, by divination. One literally calls down divine presence through certain transformation techniques.

Most feminist sorcerers use the Tarot cards, to help them to connect to their source. Tarot cards contain images of archetypal wisdom. Often just looking at them, if they are meaningfully illustrated, will bring a transformation of consciousness. Sometimes it will not. At their worst, Tarot cards offer some guidance as to our behaviour in the world. At their highest, they inspire qualities in us that we have deeply buried. A good reading can open the door for us to become who we truly are.

Tarot cards are great, because they are easily accessible and can be done as a meditation. One can draw one card and contemplate the image, bringing the knowledge the card offers, into one's life. Life is an act. You can choose a good one, or you can choose a bad one. It's completely up to you. The hardest thing is realising it. We all take our lives so seriously. This is because we are so wounded. We play being wounded dogs, howling outside the kitchen door for someone to give us some attention.

But once we have healed this damage, so that it no longer concerns us, then we are free to be anybody we choose. Our intuition will direct us as to which soul character we are currently actualising. Our clothes, our homes, even our cars - all these will become outer manifestations of who we are.

Most of the conventional tarot packs are hierarchical and dualistic - pitting one set of energies against another. Their images are very mundane. I would recommend either the Daughters of the Moon cards, or the Motherpeace set, as these have more real, inspirational images of sacred woman, for priestesses to use.

2. *Astrology*

The birthchart is a symbolic map of the heavens at the time of birth, as seen from Earth. The effect of certain planets' energies on specific areas of our lives can inspire us, or cause us to behave in certain ways. For example, if we have the spiritual, gaseous, vapourous planet Neptune in the area of work, we might be a poet. In the area of relationships, we could fall in love with God. If we have the fiery, impulsive Mars, or the speedy, quick witted Mercury, in the same areas, we will bring much energy to our work or perhaps be a communicator in some way or another - with words or music, through technology or by travel from one place to another and so on. Naturally planets fall into relationship with each other on the chart, which is known as aspect. When one planet aspects another they will affect the individual's life, making even more possibilities for pain or growth, for happiness and realisation. Each individual chart is a map. It shows the way to fullest potential if it is correctly interpreted. Sometimes the route may be right through the centre of the tension. But each person's chart is a unique blueprint, a soul-typed map to their freedom. The chart offers us a sample of the myriad possibilities that are available to each one of us in any lifetime. Within this set of possible circumstances, we can exercise free will on the matter of which life situations to choose, as well as whether or not to become free at all.

Feminist astrologers use peoples' birth charts to guide them back to their options at the time of consultation, since the beauty of a birthchart is that is only static for the moment one is born, or so it seems. For in actuality, the heavens are ever changing and are never the same twice, therefore every moment contains its own dynamic. For feminists, astrology truly becomes cosmology.

3- Teacher Plants

Healing the heart, healing the soul,
Healing the very life in me.
Healing the heart, healing the soul,
Healing the air, the earth and the sea.
Healing the heart, healing the soul,
Healing the part that is out of control.
Healing the heart, healing the soul,
Healing the part that needs to be whole.

All plants contain ingredients and essences that can affect our health, energy and well-being. However, every country contains a few that can profoundly expand consciousness. These are known as power plants, because they enable us to see and do things that we might not otherwise be able to. I prefer to call them teacher plants because they possess the key for us to enter normally unseen spheres. They can lead us to knowledge, by dissolving the veil that blocks us from direct perception of life. The filters that process and classify information as we receive it are, for a while, suspended, letting us perceive the world with awe and wonder, as if we were not separate from our object of perception.

Normally we experience life a little like watching a movie. We watch it, on a screen, outside of ourselves. This is how we see, normally. There are the mountains - they are beautiful, out there are the trees, a bird flies past the window and so on. Sometimes however, the movie is so good that we become totally engrossed in it, forgetting completely that we are sitting in the cinema watching it. We actually "lose ourselves" in it, becoming at-one with the film. Under the effect of teacher plants there is no relative distance between us and the things that come into our consciousness. We are able to connect in total fusion, to enter into communion with all that we perceive. Thus we know the trees totally because we are one with them, just as we have become one with the mountains by bonding totally with them. We are able to experience life as if there were no ending to us, or beginning to anything else - we see that we are all part of one gloriously interwoven whole.

When we see the whole world as one entity, then we see that human beings are just part of the whole function of life on earth.

"The true aim, the true evolutionary objective for humans and for all life on earth is to become one uni-mind". (Jade)

We are living in fragmentation at this time. As we are destroying the planet, so we are destroying ourselves and our life support system. Surely it is the entire function of the inhabitants of the earth to help it to continue? Yet at least half the world needs to be involved in actively healing the planet, before the balance will turn.

We can access "uni-mind" by following the energy channels of life. Everything has a life force. Teacher plants open us to pure life energy. We see the truth of the life cycle. We die, our bodies rot back into the earth. From our remains seeds sprout and grow. We are permitted a brief but necessary glimpse of the natural order of life, by opening the doorway in the brain that allows fusion with the continuum of an aspect that is normally invisible to us. Linear time no longer exists, and we are able to gain knowledge of experience that may be past, present or even future, because all time lines exist at one and the same moment. In other words we can perceive the world beyond human construction, beyond human mind. Needless to say, when we return to normal consciousness, we often do so with insight that we must then incorporate into our everyday lives, or actualise. This is why these plants are teacher plants, because they always lead us to lessons, many of which we are not normally made aware of. They are always fair. But their teaching always differs.

Usually we become blissfully happy, or even beyond happiness, in ecstasy, with teacher plants. However, there may be times when we have less pleasant experiences. This will always be due to the fact that we are in resistance to the experience and perhaps to life. This is why it is so important to prepare correctly for the experience, by choosing an appropriate time and setting for one's encounter, as well as safe, supportive company. It is useful to take plants with a guide, perhaps an experienced friend, or someone one can trust totally, because once the effects of the plants come on, one needs to be free to go into deep communion, which is what will probably happen. Teacher plants will take us into deep communion, with nature, with each other, living, or even dead, and with the divine. But first they may have to break down our blocks to entering such space, and this may involve a struggle on our part, which our minds are quite capable of winning if we choose, thus experiencing what may be called "a bad trip", or even remaining in an ego state. If we go to the experience in a state of fear, it is harder for us, so it is better to be in a state of deep meditation and connection with the divine before taking the substance and this will provide the protection and comfort that is needed and ensure a positive experience. The main thing to remember is that teacher plants are always fair, each sacred experience is always quite different from the last and just because we cannot normally enter this state at will, does not mean it is not real.

We were put on earth to evolve. Each of us incarnates in order to gain knowledge and experience. Teacher plants have been around for millennia, and despite destruction of many of their habitats, they still are. Shamans and priests have always imbibed such plants, or substances made from them, in a sacred, ceremonial manner. This is because they know that taking power plants brings one to a very religious state, characterised by blissful devotion. In such a state one can see "God" and many aspects of creation, that are not available for knowing in normal consciousness. We become open to much, much more love. Teacher plants change our frequency.

They also change our focus. Our attention can be directed to the microcosmic level. Thus we may perceive worlds within worlds. People like to call these perceptions hallucinations. But I wonder, are they the illusions. Or is the dullness and boredom of daily life, the illusion?

In the same way that we can see the patterns underlying nature, so we can see the patterns underlying human behaviour and intent, including our own. Thus an experience with teacher plants gives us the chance to change our own patterns by changing their root, which is based upon our view of ourselves and the world. We can thus do massive amounts of re-programming in a few moments, leaving us free to enjoy a happier life.

During teacher plant experiences we become open to telepathic communication. We can "speak" to anyone on the planet, alive or dead. So it is important not to have dialogue with those whom one feels can harm one and always to keep the heart open, this way one can be protected.

We see that our world is created entirely by thought, and because our sensitivity is so acute, we are able to read the intent that underpins each human activity. Thus in a state of heightened awareness we need to restrict our field of stimulus, because we can for example read the thought of the driver behind each passing car, and can therefore become misdirected. This is why a guide is recommended. Even if they don't take the plants, it is good to have someone there who can deal with "normal life", which can feel like an assault on the senses, such as someone ringing at the door, or whatever. It is worth remembering that not everyone is in the same aware state, so although the people we connect to will feel our presence, they will have to be acutely telepathically tuned themselves to become certain of the nature of your contact with them as it is happening.

Also, it is advisable to enter altered states of consciousness only when the thought fields of other people are at their lowest ebb. This of course means at night when they are peacefully sleeping. This way you can be assured of a clear space in which to adventure, where you will be undisturbed. For a few hours you can be in a world where the barriers of language and explanation dissolve, catapulting you to the infinite realms that exist beyond the normal confines of human consciousness. In this world feelings are felt at their most sensitive, music is heard at a greater depth, we can enter into the heart of every experience, hearing, seeing it anew, without the normal restrictions that operate. Our awareness travels beyond the confines of us. All of this can happen while you are just lying on your bed.

For a brief while "we" are not, and because we are not, we are so much more than usual, able for a brief respite to experience life directly, without having to perceive it through a filter and compartmentalise it through the channels of our own small understanding.

The difference between teacher plants and drugs

On the whole people do not use drugs to liberate themselves on a permanent basis from their suffering. They are not used for healing, but more for indulgence, or temporary respite from their problems, rather than to see a way through and beyond them. Many drugs are used for suppressing experience, such as pain, either physical or emotional, tiredness or other natural bodily functions. Some drugs, like heroin, are addictive in their effect, making life without them seem empty and dull, thus perpetuating their need and use. Others, like alcohol and amphetamines, increase our stimulation, but the unfortunate effect is that the sense of self as separate from others - the ego - is also heightened.

Teacher plants on the other hand, are natural substances, that are not synthesised by man, they are therefore perfectly endowed. They contain the spirit of the earth, and they are non-harmful. They are totally of the earth and contain the blueprint of human life from whence time began. They contain the right amount of active substances, so one will not overdose. Taking them triggers an interaction between you and nature. It is a very simple system, and very healing. There are no side effects, or ill effects, no addictiveness. The plants are working in accordance with the higher universe - they are part of God's army. Drugs, on the other hand, heroin, amphetamines, cocaine are part of the patriarchal army. Powerful, man-made chemicals can have a detrimental effect upon our health There is just no comparison between teacher plants and drugs. They are of a different level. The other drugs accentuate the world of mind, convincing us that we have superior faculties. They corrupt our perception, by overstimulating the ego. They lack the fine balance of teacher plants, and that's why their after-effects are so painful. After taking teacher plants one is infused with energy and inspiration and love, coming gently back to "normal" functioning, but bringing the vision back for incorporation into one's life.

Chapter 4
Towards enlightenment.

"Enlightenment is infinite, because of this you can only go towards it. We are all seekers. We seek knowledge. To say that everybody in this lifetime can be enlightened means that everybody can get on the path to enlightenment. There can never be a master, only a guide". (Jade.)

There is such a pressure amongst spiritual seekers to reach enlightenment. This creates hierarchy and desire. We all want to become enlightened, and begin to compare ourselves to others who say they are enlightened, resulting in feelings of hopelessness, because we feel we will never get there. We evolve eternally, but we don't reach an end goal that we can call enlightenment. Therefore there is really no such thing as enlightenment. Maybe people need to have enlightenment as an attainable goal because they need a goal to grab hold of? But this is the patriarchal emphasis. We are therefore free to stop the competition to reach enlightenment.

"This is not to knock those seers who claim to be enlightened. If anything it is to bring them together. For those who seek the truth, there are only parallels. We are the eternals. True enlightenment is ongoing". (Jade).

Women practicing paths that promise to lead to enlightenment need to re-evaluate existing ideas about enlightenment. Those women who are following teachings that have as their goal the state of enlightenment or realisation, need to become aware that there may be no such destination.

Whilst I do not deny the need for a teacher, I bring into question the idea of a state of enlightenment which is definitive. Perhaps there is no end to the road of becoming? Just more and more expansion. Eternally and infinitely!

Neither is there anything intrinsically wrong with spiritual practice. Especially if it is therapeutic and enhances the life state of each practicing individual. One's faith and happiness just grows and grows. But this is the point. There can be no goal. There is just more and more unfolding. After all who can say when a woman is enlightened? And if she becomes enlightened, does she still keep practicing her faith? Surely life must just grow and grow?

The main message for women today is for us to broaden the scope of our love. Yes, we have the ability to love, love is our power and our strength. But our greatest mistake is to love too narrowly, too possessively, thus our love is not the truly healing force that evolution now dictates it must become. We must develop the capacity for universal love. The only way we can truly find the power and strength we need to heal ourselves, the Earth and all her creatures, is by seeking and finding the power of the absolute, the infinite, the one, God - whatever you want to call the great creative force that permeates everything in the universe. By immersing ourselves within that energy we will become whole and healed. Everything we do will be safe and correct, and spring only from divine will. We must learn to distinguish between our will and God's will. Only by the power of the latter can we be assured of true, unchanging and ever increasing happiness.

Ecstatica is the new high state of being for women. It is the new space that we are going to be inhabiting more and more and more. I say new, although it is really quite ancient, because the technology to reach this state of being, the simple wholistic technology, is being taught rapidly and widespreadedly. Keep searching and searching until you know that you have found what it is that you were looking for, and even when you have found it still keep on searching, for there is more. More love, more power. Love is eternal, it just goes on and on.

FEMINIST PRAYERS AND GUIDANCE

Ecstatica

Feminist Prayers and Guidance

Prayer to find a resting place.
Prayer for the will to do my act of power.
Affirmation of positivity and faith.
Prayer to the Creatrix of life.
You have answered me.
The only thing that matters.
Manifesting your destiny.
You don't need anyone to validate you.
Holy Woman.
Be not quick to judge others.
On suffering a setback.
On giving up our attachments.
Listen to your tone.
I humbly pray.
Love.
Help me to know your will.
Just switch on the love current.
Clarity.
Magic.
Accept yourself in all your beauty
Let out your witch.
I am a priestess of life.
You are God's love.
Being present.
Before you start the day. Meditate to find the answer.

The wisest choices may not always be the easiest options.
Prayer.
Trust.
Focus.
The choice is yours.
Help me to stop the pain

Prayer to find a resting place.

We are a new tribe and we need a new home. Somewhere where we can be large enough lifed. We need to be somewhere, where we can be ourselves, while we wait for the other bits of our tribe to join us, as one day we know they will. In the meantime, we need somewhere to hang out. It is time to start living now, no longer waiting hopelessly for life to begin. It must be a beautiful and peaceful place; a place to recharge, with the energy of nature, our batteries that are so run down by the assault of city life, with its heavy angriness, people always just on the verge of exploding. This is no safe place to bring up little children!

I ask to be provided with a house, safe for us and the children. Large enough to live in and to create in. It should be sunny and spacious and verging onto land where we can walk in freedom and commune with wildlife and nature. May we now have some true beauty in our lives to feed our starved souls and to help us to create and store the energy we will need for our future tasks of freeing and liberating ourselves and others.

May we now be provided with a space to heal ourselves and the children. May they be nurtured and protected, but also given a sense of decency and the true and important values in life. I long to be at home in a whole and balanced life, and I give thanks for the tremendous bounty I have already received.

INTERNATIONAL WOMEN'S DAY 1993
(March 8th-also my 41st birthday)

Prayer for the will to do my act of power.

There is no time to get miserable, there is only time to focus; to focus on your great work and to complete it, for this is your act of power as a woman. It is the only thing that will take away the suffering, the longing, the agonising over the meaning of life. That is the discipline of doing something and letting it carry you beyond thought, beyond suffering. To believe in your work and to do it, against the adversity of your daily life as a woman, against the resistance of your own soul, your lack of faith in yourself. Just carry on, keep up, and with each day your work will grow, your faith in yourself will increase and your load will lighten!

Ecstatica

Affirmation of positivity and faith

I have decided that I am not going to worry about anything. What I mean is I am not going to feel fear. I am not going to indulge the fear that intelligent women feel when they begin to think of the truth of their lives, in relation to the type of lives patriarchally programmed women lead. I trust that my life is in order. That it accords with cosmic law. I trust that I am under the total guidance and protection of God.

Prayer to the Creatrix of life

Speak to me directly oh creatrix of life. Greatest power that rules the universe and the cosmos. I look everywhere for an answer but I can no longer rely on outside sources and I ask you to speak to my heart and my wisdom. I am open to what you have to say. There is no book yet written that can speak of your holy splendour.

Representations of you are but mere icons and by their form, limit our perception of you. You are the highest of the high, no words can do you justice. I cast out to you with the sincere feelings in my heart in the hope that you will offer me your protection and your guidance, which I will trust to lead me to my liberation even though I may not understand it.

I do not know what you are, but I do know that I am missing you and I beg you to take me into your energy and comfort.

You have answered me.

You have just told me to let go - to surrender and relax. You have said that if I simply STOP, you will surround me with some of your awesome power. Then despair and sadness will evaporate like a damp, grey cloud under the fierce heat of the sun.

The only thing that matters.

The only thing that matters when mentally processing what has occurred after interacting with people who can affect one, is to run to one's religious practice. For it is in the silence of the heart that one will be able to free oneself from blame, pain or attachment. (December 9th 1992).

Manifesting your destiny

Women need to make an act of power to glean energy from our life and surroundings. First of all we need to define our act of power. Then we need to build up the strength, to garner the energy to make the commitment to focus on our target. For a once weak person like myself, this process can take years of refinement, gradually facing up to oneself, no longer deluding oneself about our abilities, gradually, gradually building up. Then making the chances and grabbing them, for fear they will not come twice.

What do I want out of it all? Why absolute freedom of course. Freedom from suffering and to be happy. The sort of freedom that can probably only come with death. The freedom that comes from having attended to everything. Having tied up all your spiritual and material ends. So on I go, each day adjusting and refining my life, which is the only real work of art I possess.

You don't need anyone to validate you

You don't need anyone to validate you. You don't need me to give you a certificate at the end of your sacred studies. You will be your own validator - the one who decides whether you have increased yourself to your best abilities.

Such knowledge comes from inside one, from the intuition, which says, "OK. I'm me now, the best I can be. I have become the totality of myself".

Life is not a holier than thou competition. No one has the spiritual prerogative to pass judgement on another's religiousness. One's relationship with God is a purely personal thing which does not hold to fixed criteria. You are what you are. A totally unique being, therefore you cannot be awarded a certificate by anyone else but you. If you insist I will give you a certificate on which will be inscribed:-

The Centre for Sacred Women's Studies awards you a certificate of excellence for being you.

But it is meaningless, because you and only you will know whether you feel like a shit or on top of the world.

Ecstatica

Holy woman

I am a holy woman. But I embrace more than one religion. There are in all traditions good things and bad things. As a woman of today I am religious, but I am inspired by all religions. I look for the core of universal truth at the heart of each of them. They all lead to the one source of all creation, which is accessible when I become my higher self.

I can be in this state of my higher me with Krishna, Jesus, Mary, Tara, Shiva, Buddha, Guru Nanak. Gods and Goddesses from all traditions inspire me to worship of the one God, which is the sacred flow of life as created, upheld and always supported by the merciful, compassionate creator.

For me, holiness is found within every religion and all religions. Therefore I object to being judged by patriarchal men and women with mean faces who think they are religious and I am not, and because they feel like shit, they want all the world to feel bad. You can be part of an established church, but it doesn't mean you are religious. Religiousness shows in the mind and in the purity of one's thoughts. In the decency of one's behaviour, in the extent of one's compassion, in the amount of one's lovingness. You can attend synagogue and attend temple and get on your knees and pray. But if you are not sincere and you do not really care, because you are wallowing in self-hatred, then those prayers lack content and passion and fall on deaf ears, and your life will not change one bit and you will be doomed to suffering.

The way is there for everyone. As soon as you start to follow it, to obey the dictates of the evolution of your soul you will feel better. Then you will be religious, and your holiness, your spirituality will be equal to the highest Buddha. As that great healer John Lennon said, "**All You Need Is Love**".

Be not quick to judge others

Be not quick to judge others. You may be wrong. Besides it will alienate you not only from them, but also from yourself. Whilst you reassure yourself of your righteousness, you will not bring out the best in them. See their anger, see their pain, see their negativity, but only witness it and be neutral. Do not attach to their suffering. Also see their beauty, see their divine essence, call to their higher natures, call to their hearts, talk to their spirits and not to their minds. Pray for their happiness, talk deep and in subtle ways.

Then the truly pleasant surprise is, everyone becomes interesting, everyone becomes innocent and childlike. Call to them softly from where you are, show them a glimpse of your heaven, but do not let their anger cause you to abandon it, to lose your faith and belief. Your heaven is real - you worked hard for it and it's as real as their pain, their suffering, their illusion. It is just the better choice, so protect it with your life, but share it with them so they can see that it is possible to change their pain into joy too. Anyone can reach their own heaven in their lifetime, whoever they are, whatever their life tasks and obligations. Heaven is where impeccability is. Let yourself truly grow up.

On suffering a setback

There will be times when you suffer what feels like a setback to your progress. You will have felt like you were really becoming free of your old painful patterns. Then one day you will feel that it has all slipped away from you as your negativity returns and all your gains feel lost. As if you had not changed at all from that old self. Please know that you have not really slipped back at all. You have not slipped up anywhere. These patterns are merely re-surfacing in order to catch your attention, to test your faith and strength and endurance. That is all. They are there to help you to confront and bring attention to the way these brain patterns operate, and suddenly switch you from being your loving high self to a dark and moody self. Do not panic. Do not judge yourself. Do not be harsh. Know that this is just the way it goes. If the patterns do not emerge, then we cannot become aware of them and if we do not become aware of them, then we cannot change them.

On giving up our attachments

It takes courage to give up the external props that we use to help us through each day. We need to muster our faith to believe that we truly can be at our best without anything outside of our own being. Many of us live as addicts in bondage to an external stimulus that we believe helps us through our lives. When are we going to believe in ourselves? That our own bodies contain all the power we need to live in ecstasy? We need to realise that ecstasy comes from within ourselves, and is the result of our engaging our wills fully in creative activity. The only high which is reliable, constant, is the naturally generated high which comes from clearing and cleaning our lives, in order that we become true open channels to receive the flow of divine goodness.

Listen to your tone

Take a deep breath - let go of the tension. Let go of your pain. Maybe your pain is "God's love in disguise", come to remind you of your true mission to serve the greater whole and in so doing free yourself like a soaring eagle.

What is your pain? Your nagging voice, your needy voice, your sad and sorry voice, your mean and moody voice, your dull and drained voice?

Listen to your tone. How do you sound, even though you are not speaking. Listen with your neutral brave self - do not be afraid, or guilty of what you hear with your inner ear. Do not judge yourself, for it is not the true you who is down, just the part of the self that feeds on outward stimuli, on outward needs.

Open yourself in all innocence. Let the harsh part of you, your personality, out. Just let it fly, and open your heart totally to the compassionate creator. If you are sincere and you truly want to change your behaviour, then take forgiveness from the unending source and wash your soul over with the merciful compassion heaven bestows, that is always present on earth.

Because heaven is here now, for everyone, for all who have the ears to listen and the heart to feel.

I humbly pray

I humbly pray with all my heart for no more hurt or pain. I sit in my chair, or on the floor and I pray with passion and caring for an end to all suffering. I pray with all my heart, my body and my soul.

At the same time I know that I do not need to take on all the suffering of humanity and animals. I give and I take in balance and I am always careful to do no harm.

I am sincerely trying to change my life.

Love.

I offer wholehearted love. I think no ill of you, although I am aware of your faults. I always help you by staying neutral, by loving you, seeing your true essence as well as your negative self.

I wait for you to connect to me in my honesty as I open myself to you. I will not force you to join me, nor put out thoughts of doubt about you or myself. I am always here if you need me to give you a chance to show you that I care.

Meanwhile I know you will feel my love for you and hope you will be willing to make a commitment to me now.

Help me to know your will

I don't need success or fame. I did once want it but now it is no longer so important for me to gain recognition. However what I do need is the freedom to live out the reality choices I wish to make. This freedom comes at a price and requires certain life criteria (chess moves on the game board of life), to be fulfilled.

I want to work towards my freedom. I will do whatever I have to do to secure it - if one can secure freedom - and I humbly ask for you, oh natural law, to throw up the opportunities for me to work off my karma and to free myself of all obligations, so that I may be joyous of spirit and infused with your glow. So that you may grant me personal power, which comes from doing your will.

Help me only to know your will. The rest you can leave up to me.

Just switch on the love current

The best I can do is to LOVE. To stay loving and open. Now at last I have discovered that it is correct to love. That it is your will, oh creator, greatest power, to LOVE.

I have in the past felt blocked to give my wholehearted love. I have switched off my love flow current, feeling as if it was not right to love. As if you could love too much. I have failed to extend my heart fully to everyone, because I felt my love was in short supply and would not be replenished. I felt people were no good and so I couldn't trust them.

Unconditional love means seeing they are no good and still loving them. Or seeing the good in them whilst not letting the bad influence you.

Clarity

I accept that the things that happen to me are the direct result of my thoughts and visualisations (positive or negative). Clarity is my ability to trace these linkages from their root in my mind, to the results of its activity in my life.

Magic

Magic is my ability to change the cause and hence the effect of my limiting beliefs. I can create a reality that mirrors my inner state that is within my power to affect. Magic is a mixture of your (God's) will and my choices. If I find the point of alignment between the two this is where MAGIC is.

Accept yourself in all your beauty

When the tao is personalised according to the people of that time, the deities will reflect the qualities of the time. Patriarchal societies personify their deities according to values of patriarchal goodness (morality). Unworthy, ungodly behaviour has been defined in patriarchal terms. There are male gods and there are female goddesses, but all have been created from the mind of man. Mary was a saint. Popular myth would have it that she was also a virgin. But she was a mother. Something derogatory is being said here about sex and sainthood.

Sometimes we can no longer live up to the standards that have been falsely attributed to the deities. It is no longer spiritually correct for us to do so. Keeping up a model of purity, when we no longer subscribe to it, can cause us many problems. When we realise what "God" is actually saying to us is, **"accept yourself in all your beauty"**, you will see that you and God mirror each other. As you are, so God is.

If you bleed it is God.
If you have a womb, it is God.
If you sometimes feel like eating meat
And you do, it is God.

If your body gives you pleasure
And you feel it,
it is one of the loving gifts of God.

Ecstatica

You are God
And God is you.
If you personalise the Tao
Don't forget the body.

You are the body of God
And God's body is just like you
Soft and warm and round
With bouncy breasts and all.

Let out your witch.

Let out your witch.
Let her fly out of you.
The power of her heart will rule.

Are you hiding your witch? Is it for fear of disapproval? Are you frightened of the fathers' judgement? The
mothers' fear of you? Are you scared by your own wildness?

Stop and think about it. Your wildness is a part of
God's love. God loves your witch, because your witch is the
one who is connected to God's creation - nature. Your witch
is the healer, the one who can tune to God's rhythms and
learn to interpret God's message and read God's flow and
hence know how to use it for good. And it could only be for
good, so strong is the power of your heart.

Trust yourself totally. Accept yourself in all your forms.

I am a priestess of life

It is great that women have been allowed to ordain as Christian priests. But I am a priestess too. My ordination consists of years of self-motivated study, contemplation, prayer, devotion and faith, which I have done alone and with the loving support of my family.

I am a priestess of the Sacred Women's tradition. A priestess of no fixed faith, only that faith is love. Yet a priestess nevertheless. A priestess of life.

I chant and I pray fervently and passionately, casting my heart out to God and humanity. But I remain unconfined to any particular church or teachings because God is all one. God is all faiths and all teachings. At their core is God.

God is every religion and every race. God is both genders. God is mother and father and lover and child. God is above and below, within and without. The whole of the universe is God and infused with God's love.

You are God's love

Are you infused with the power of your own life? Are you in control of your own destiny? Is your will engaged in your life?

Your life is your ship to steer and you can make it as beautiful and as as sacred as you like.

You can make each day holier than the last.

Open yourself to the soaring passions of wild-hearted woman as she bursts out of the bonds of patriarchy, those spine-chilling, sickening, numbing, deadening, dulling waves of sucked-inward emotions that we feel.

Burst forth, cut free, through those veils of nothingness and come into the vibrating, pulsating, happy energy of life that is always here, always present in every moment of our lives. Just stop and step into joy.

Trust yourself. You really are changing your life. Breaking down your negative behaviour patterns, exhorting yourself to do better each day. **NO GUILT. NO BLAME. NO SHAME.**

You are love. You are God's love.

Being present

The only hope I have of stopping my pain is to stop my dialogue. To come wholly into the present and to concentrate on what I'm doing. I will simply watch my thoughts as they form like waves upon the sea shore and then pass again, trying always to return to full attention on the present.

Before you start the day

Before you do anything else in the morning, you need to let go completely of everything you are holding on to, so that you do not do anything under stress. You need to make time for a meditative practice after first drinking a glass of water to cleanse impurities from your body.

Then after that, and only when you have totally surrendered yourself to your healing practice, and eliminated all thoughts, pressures, lists, will you be ready to start the day.

Meditate to find the answer

Your mind will lead you a merry dance. Thinking about your choices will only make them seem more complicated. One should meditate to find the answer to one's problems. In the wisdom of one's heart and the clarity that comes from silencing the mental chatter you will find your answer.

The wisest choices may not always be the easiest options.

I trust you to help me to make the right choices. Choices based not on fear and doubt, but on courage and wisdom. What I am choosing now is in the name of power not attachment. Love will never die.

I trust that I will be guided to the best choices, which may not always be the easiest options.

Prayer

Prayer is the ability to sit quietly, to breathe deeply and to offer yourself wholeheartedly to the creator as a force for good.

Prayer is the energy you store up and use in order to live your life creatively.

Trust

Trust is letting go. It can only happen if you have "grown ups" around you, who can take over from you for a while so that you can exit normal space/time and go into sacred space for some regeneration. You need to know that these friends are competent to handle the interests of your normal life, so that you can just go into bliss.

Focus

The world is full of exciting things to do. We need to concentrate our energies on one task or project at a time, lest our power becomes dissipated in the myriad mountain of life's possibilities.

By focusing on our chosen path, we can go ever deeper into its core as our consciousness grows and hence we see it in new ways all the time. Therefore, although it is only one path, it has no limits and our liberation will be found deep within its centre.

The choice is yours

Each moment of your life offers you the power to make a choice. You can choose to act or react, negatively or positively.

What are the factors that cause us to choose negatively? Why do we choose to behave badly when we could equally act with maturity and dignity?

We need to look at the history behind our reaction, behind our negative choice. Our negative choice represents a choice for self-hatred and a choice made from our own anger.

Ask why are we angry? What needs are not being met? Are they valid needs, or is it just old programming?

Learn to take a breath before reacting. In that space comes a pause. Use the pause to consciously decide your response.

Help me to stop the pain

We have to learn how to stop perpetuating the pain. Letting our rage fly out at innocent targets. When we see someone in a state of rage venting their frustration and pain on another, what should we do? Do we stand and look? Do we intervene?

So far the only answer I have been able to find to this is to send a strong psychic message of my anger and disapproval, then to go home and let go of it, by chanting and contemplating, sending my love to the victim and the oppressor, because they are both caught up on the wheel of suffering.

If I intervene, I may bear the brunt of 50 years or more patriarchally embedded anger. Will this angry person not think that I am judging her too? Is my own righteous rage not more powerful, than her unrighteous anger? But I don't want to get killed for my troubles.

So I don't really have the answer yet. This sort of pain and frustration goes on all around me, so when I encounter it how am I to cope without letting it ruin the day and depress me? If I witness this suffering, does it not then become my problem too, as I am involved?

Everyone has free will. That is the hardest thing for a healer to accept, when witnessing harm being done. But we are not God, only agents of God, and we must not intervene in the divine plan, whereby each person lives out their own life. If it is appropriate for me to offer help and encouragement I will do so, but I will not take on the pain of the whole universe. Meanwhile I humbly ask for a way of dealing with the pain of witnessing and feeling the suffering of others.